T0383656

"*Ableism in Education* provides a necessary counternarrative to the lives of disabled students and their families. Education scholar Gillian Parekh writes of how ableism as an ideology serves to structure the ways in which we think of, and work with, students who present as not having met predetermined indicators of social and intellectual development. With this critical and valuable work, Parekh makes the indispensable link between ableism, classism, and racism, detailing how these and other forms of discrimination operate as barriers to education and schooling. A must read for educators, clinicians, and parents."

—**Carl E. James**, author of *Colour Matter: Essays on the Experiences, Education, and Pursuits of Black Youth*

"Dr. Gillian Parekh has delivered an important new book that centers disability in the fight for justice in schools. With a balance of historical context, current research, and theoretical depth, this book provides a critical entry into understanding how we construct ability and disability and enact ableism in our current educational practice. The book also provides a way forward with guidance for reflection throughout the book, as well as for practice that centers the experience of disabled students."

—**Kathryn Underwood**, Professor, Director of the Inclusive Early Childhood Service System Project, Toronto

"*Ableism in Education: Rethinking School Practices and Policies* is an essential read for all educators in public education. Dr. Parekh provides a direct but simple alternative path forward in rethinking the purpose of public education from one largely instrumental in reinforcing societies' existing inequities and oppression to one that could serve as a critical platform for social justice and opportunity for the historically most marginalized and economically disadvantaged communities and people. In rethinking common notions of 'ability' and 'disability'— both central to public education's mission—Parekh breathes life into a different way to perceive what it is to know something, for whom, and for what. In so doing, she offers new possibilities for how educators and the education system alike might work."

—**Dr. David Hagen Cameron**, Senior Manager Research and Development, Toronto District School Board

Ableism in Education

Rethinking School Practices and Policies

Equity and Social Justice in Education Series

Cheryl E. Matias and Paul C. Gorski, Series Editors

Routledge's Equity and Social Justice in Education series is a publishing home for books that apply critical and transformative equity and social justice theories to the work of on-the-ground educators. Books in the series describe meaningful solutions to the racism, white supremacy, economic injustice, sexism, heterosexism, transphobia, ableism, neoliberalism, and other oppressive conditions that pervade schools and school districts.

Equity-Centered Trauma-Informed Education
Alex Shevrin Venet

Social Studies for a Better World: An Anti-Oppressive Approach for Elementary Educators
Noreen Naseem Rodríguez and Katy Swalwell

Learning and Teaching While White: Antiracist Strategies for School Communities
Jenna Chandler-Ward and Elizabeth Denevi

Public School Equity: Educational Leadership for Justice
Manya C. Whitaker

Ableism in Education: Rethinking School Practices and Policies
Gillian Parekh

Ableism in Education
Rethinking School
Practices and Policies

Gillian Parekh

Routledge
Taylor & Francis Group

NEW YORK AND LONDON

Note to Readers: Models and/or techniques described in this volume are illustrative or are included for general informational purposes only; neither the publisher nor the author(s) can guarantee the efficacy or appropriateness of any particular recommendation in every circumstance. As of press time, the URLs displayed in this book link or refer to existing sites. The publisher and author are not responsible for any content that appears on third-party websites.

Cover design: Lauren Graessle
Cover image: ©Adrienne Bresnahan/Getty Images

First published in 2022 by W. W. Norton

Published in 2024 by Routledge
605 Third Avenue, New York, NY 10158
4 Park Square, Milton Park, Abingdon, Oxon, OX14 4RN

Routledge is an imprint of the Taylor & Francis Group, an informa business

©2022 Gillian Parekh

The right of Gillian Parekh to be identified as author of this work has been asserted in accordance with sections 77 and 78 of the Copyright, Designs and Patents Act 1988.

Library of Congress Cataloging-in-Publication Data
A catalog record for this title has been requested

ISBN: 9781032597126 (pbk)
ISBN: 9781032677965 (ebk)

DOI: 10.4324/9781032677965

For Mom, Dad, and T, my first teachers, who continue to challenge ableism and push for systemic change.

Contents

Part I
Thinking Through Ability, Disability, and Ableism

Part II
How Students Are Organized by Ability

Part III
Practical Strategies for the School and Classroom

Acknowledgments

Just as it takes a village to raise a child, it takes a community to write a book. Many thanks to Dr. Paul C. Gorski for the invitation to be a part of his vision for an equity series that could empower educators and effect change in schools. Thank you to Carol Collins and W. W. Norton for their continuing support throughout the writing process. Thank you to Dr. Robert S. Brown for your tireless support, for always being up to the challenge, and for your ongoing mentorship. Thank you to Dr. Isabel Killoran for reviewing my many drafts and excerpts, and for still taking my late-night and weekend calls and questions. Thank you to Dr. Jessica Vorstermans for your friendship and for talking through the tough bits. Many heartfelt thanks to all the students, educators, and administrators who gave up their time to speak with our research team and to share their insights. I have learned so much.

Thank you to the movers and shakers in public education who produce research and use research to better the conditions in schools, Dr. David Cameron, Samuel Zheng, Janet O'Reilly, Maria Yau, Amie Presley, Erhan Sinay, Ian Allison, Dr. Anne Seymour, Dr. Uton Robinson, Dr. Monday Gala, Alison Gaymes San Vicente, Ramon San Vicente, Karen Murray, Jason To, Salima Kassam, Peggy Blair, Chris Conley, Dr. Brendan Browne, Dr. Jack Nigro, Roula Anastasakos, Sally Erling, Margaret Douglin, Lisa Newton, Rob Caruso, Lisa Rosolen, George Tam, Dr. Cosmin Marmureanu, and everyone working within the Research and Development Department at the TDSB. Thank you to the visionaries who generously shared your knowledge and expertise and helped shape my understanding of what equity means in schools, including Dr. Rubén Gaztambide-Fernández, Dr. Nirmala Erevelles, Dr. Elizabeth J. Grace, Dr. Kathryn Underwood, Dr. Carl E. James, Dr. Susan Winton, Dr. Vidya Shah, Dr. Rachel da Silva Gorman, Dr. Karen Robson, Dr. Natalie Coulter, and Dr. Harry Smaller. Thank you to George Martell, who knew, way back, where I needed to go and helped steer me in the right direction. Thanks to Dr. Gary Bunch, Dr. Gordon Porter and the Inclusive Education Canada team, as well as to the Canada Research Center on Inclusive Education for your community and leadership.

To my SEEDS community, you've been there for me more than you know. To my friends, thank you for checking in and getting me out. To my family here in the big city, thank you for listening, for your patience, your lightness and laughter, and for bringing me tea when you knew it was most needed. To my family back on the East Coast, thank you for allowing me to share your stories, for giving me my stories, and for journeying with me. Lastly, this writing and research was made possible in large part due to the generous funding from the Social Science and Humanities Research Council of Canada as well as the Canada Research Chair program.

Introduction

"It is not at all surprising to find the notion of ability being used to compare and rank students, given the institutional function of school has long been precisely that."

—LADWIG & MCPHERSON, 2017, P. 8

If you've ever been to school, various aspects of your ability have been measured and used to inform decisions about where you "fit" and what opportunities you deserve. Some of those decisions may have felt fair, others not so much. But those decisions likely have a lot to do with where you are today. In fact, how your ability was perceived in school and the opportunities you were afforded or denied may be critical factors determining your current employment status, your access to healthcare, housing, and income. But what even is "ability"? How and who decides what counts as ability and who should be considered able, unable, or disabled? And how might other factors, such as gender, economic privilege, racial identity, or immigration status influence how ability is perceived?

Ability is a critical factor in schools, and yet, in discussions on equity and social justice in education, ability and ableism are rarely addressed. It's not easy because ability is explicitly central to the aims and the function of schooling. Critically examining ability means critically examining the core values upon which education is built. Schools rely on understandings of ability to rank, sort, and organize students into pathways and programs as well as align students with different kinds of educational opportunities. Student ability is often a central theme in parent–teacher interviews and a primary concern shared between educators as to how best assess and support students who may appear to be struggling. So how do critical educators problematize issues of equity and ableism, when so many of their day-to-day activities include engaging, shaping, assessing, measuring, and reporting on ability?

Schools are important in teaching children and youth key skills they will use throughout their lifetime. Students have the right to education and the right to learn academic skills (United Nations, 1966; OHRC, 2019). Promoting the development of abilities, for instance, the ability to read, solve math problems, understand political, biological, and economic systems, engage in language, how to think critically, and so forth is important. However, ability in schools is used in many ways, including decisions on how to organize students and allocate resources and opportunities. As ability is so central to schooling—and as schooling plays such a big role in shaping our understanding of ability, ability-based decisions often appear logical, rational, natural, or neutral. They are not. Ability, and how schools respond to ability, are highly constructed and vulnerable to bias. For instance, schools are not allowed to discriminate or exclude students from general education based on race or class, yet many forms of racial and class discrimination enacted in schools are justified by citing students' *perceived* ability (Reid & Knight, 2006). In fact, we have entire systems set up to facilitate the organization and exclusion of students based on perceptions of ability. Schools tend to promote notions of ability that privilege white, middle-class children. This is not new. Special education populations have historically been and continue to be disproportionately racialized, from lower income homes, LGBTQ2S+, and multilingual learners, often with little or no evidence of pathology or impairment (Artiles et al., 2010; Connor, 2017; Reid & Knight, 2006).

How schools respond to and organize students by ability results in very real, lifelong social and economic consequences for students and their families. These consequences can include sustained generational poverty; social and political exclusion; income, housing, and food insecurity; and long-term health implications. Organizational decisions based on ability can have profound impacts on disabled students and students constructed as disabled. But their experiences of exclusion based on ability are not isolated from their experiences of other forms of discrimination. Therefore, when we think about disability justice, we need to conceptualize it as in solidarity with racial, economic, sexual, health, and class justice. This book examines the "tyranny of ability" (Parekh, 2017) in schools and its role in racial and class oppression, as well as how equity-seeking educators can survive and thrive in systems that, at times, work against the values of justice.

Thinking About Ability in Schools: Disability Studies in Education

Although there are many forms of ability, in schools, ability is often considered to be synonymous with intellectual or cognitive ability (Ladwig & McPherson, 2017). Ability is assessed in a variety of ways both inside and outside of schools, and many of these measures can be fraught with bias. However, I would argue that assumptions around students' ability and future capacity are made long before students are formally assessed. I would also argue that the trigger point for formal assessment or intervention may vary depending on students' social identities. For instance, the point for which a white, female student is suspected to have an impairment might be far different than for her racialized, male classmate. In addition to race and gender, immigration, language, class, sexuality—and their associated forms of discrimination (e.g., racism, sexism, classism, xenophobia, homophobia)—collude to shape perceptions of students' ability in schools as well as to determine which interventions are deemed appropriate.

Disability studies in education (DSE) is a growing field of study that examines how ability and disability are constructed, understood, and responded to in schools. DSE is the integration of disability studies into educational spaces, schooling practices, and tensions around best-practices to support students (Gabel, 2005). DSE scholars and/or practitioners are sometimes considered DSE-grounded educators or critical special educators (Connor, 2019). Offering a counter narrative to special education and ability-grouping practices, Connor (2019) offers the following guiding tenets.

> *The tenets of DSE are to engage in research, policy, and action that*
> - *contextualize disability within political and social spheres*
> - *privilege the interest, agendas, and voices of people labeled with disability/disabled people*
> - *promote social justice, equitable and inclusive educational opportunities, and full and meaningful access to all aspects of society for people labeled with disability/disabled people*
> - *assume competence and reject deficit models of disability (p. 11)*

In addition to these tenets, DSE explores how intersecting discriminations, colonialism, and white supremacy shape historical and current notions of normalcy. DSE examines organizational decisions and ability-based practices, such as special education, academic streaming, and specialized programming, and considers how these school-based practices contribute to the ongoing social and cultural reproduction and stratification of privilege in broader society. DSE explores how ability and ableism in school is used to justify the maintenance of generational poverty and systemic racism by determining what kind of access students have to a future of their choosing.

I have long been interested in ability, disability, and schooling. When my brother was born with cerebral palsy, my parents took on the role of fierce advocates for his inclusion in school. Observing again and again how his contributions were diminished and disregarded and how his repeated exclusions in school were justified by his disability made me wonder *for whom and under what conditions* do schools decide to include. As a youth, I, too, struggled in school. At age 9, I was diagnosed with anxiety and clinical depression. In my teens, I was in and out of psychiatric care and would spend months at a time in hospital-run day programs. As a result, I missed a lot of school and eventually dropped out. My journey back would be a long and complicated one.

One of the reasons I became interested in DSE is that both my brother and I found school challenging, albeit in very different ways.

My brother required physical accommodations such as access to technology, to an educational assistant, and mobility supports. In my case, I was that student who didn't show up to class, and even when physically present, I failed tests, found it hard to focus, forgot assignments, and did my best to avoid any attention from teachers. When I'd asked for accommodations, I was told they would make me "soft," that accommodations would allow my illness to "win," and they would leave me unprepared for the "real world." Sentiments I continue to hear in education today.

Another reason for my interest in DSE is that I believe that schools perpetuate the notion that disability equates *brokenness*. Whether the damage is perceived as physical, intellectual, emotional, or psychological, far too often students are put in the position to seek, compliantly accept, and commit to fixing what is "wrong" with them. For my brother and me, the specter of normalization was ever present. What did we need to do to behave, feel, and exist closer to normalcy? The continuous focus in both our personal and academic lives was on rehabilitation, therapy and "cure." These goals led me to believe that being disabled meant being an unfinished project, one that *never* fully arrives into being, as forever remaining *damaged* or *incomplete*.

DSE challenges individualistic notions of disability, where the "problem" lies within the person, and instead examines the social and environmental conditions that produce disablement. In my experience, interventions and treatment rarely considered environmental conditions, but would instead ask (require) me to acknowledge (admit/confess) that the problem was within myself and urge (demand) my commitment (compliance) to fixing it. Even when I was younger, I felt that individual-only approaches to treatment were largely ineffective; after all, I had been undergoing treatment for years with no success. Regardless, I still believed that disability was an entirely individual issue. Both in school and in treatment, I had been repeatedly told that I needed to pull myself together—to "get over it" (said with deepest empathy, of course), and that if I couldn't dig deep and get it together, then I was weak and to blame. Although it hurt tremendously, I embodied this belief. I embodied ableism, and it skewed my entire perception of disability and early approaches to teaching.

Disability and Approaches to Teaching

My first education job was as a special education teacher. When my brother was a student, my parents fought for full inclusion. As a result, he had a personal educational assistant by his side throughout the day and a computer, in the days when few students had computers. For most of his public school education, there were very few students in his classes with visible disability. Flanked by an adult, a service dog, and enough gear to fill a small classroom, developing social relations with peers was challenging. And although his academics were solid, enough so that he would eventually enter graduate school, he often felt a deep sense of loneliness. Therefore, in my teaching, I was determined to not only consider academics but create opportunities for students to experience a real sense of belonging, to reap the benefits of being in community, and to develop authentic peer relationships.

After a week of interviews, I found myself sitting in the principal's office of a school designated only for students identified with rare and complex disabilities. The administrator spoke to the school's emphasis on fostering relationships; on social development and friendships; advocacy and making sure that the students at the school had access to the best resources, technology, and services the city could offer. I knew, then, that this was exactly where I wanted to be and was elated when the job offer came through.

The structure of the school was far different than I had anticipated, and I relied heavily on the guidance and mentorship of many trusted and experienced staff. After a while, the broken schedules, the multiple specialists cycling through the classroom, the late arrivals and early departures of busses all became routine. There were, of course, some challenges, but most were generated at a structural level. For example, the organization of transportation and schedules sometimes made it difficult to focus on academics. But the staff were dedicated and passionate, and the administration promoted advocacy and disability rights. Even though the school community was small and isolated, students fostered meaningful relationships, played pranks, and shared jokes among each other and the staff.

At the time, the school's ethos aligned with my conception of disability. In addition to an emphasis on community, the school prioritized access to physical, cognitive, and communication therapies. My role as a teacher was, in part, to facilitate the rehabilitative and normalization goals directed by professional services at and through the school. As my own experience of disability had been framed by rehabilitation and therapy, I happily participated and supported this pedagogical direction. To me, student enrollment was symbolic of a radical choice families had made for the betterment of their children's education and I was excited to be a part.

However, it became apparent that placement in this school wasn't a choice for all families. In fact, I found out that many families had likely been given only two options: pursuing schooling with *no* support for their child, or placement in our school. To many families, our school was representative of complete system exclusion. Due to how resources were organized and allocated across the system, many of our students had not been allowed to attend school in their communities with their friends or siblings. I also found out that having ever been placed at our school carried a significant stigma and all but ensured that students would face a future of exclusion and resistance to their inclusion elsewhere. It became clear to me that many of our students, even our most promising academic students, would not be moving onto high schools or programs that would grant them a secondary-school diploma. They would instead graduate with a certificate, largely ensuring that students' prospects for college or any tertiary education were nonexistent. This is when I began questioning the role of special education schools and the logics of organizing students by ability.

Reorienting My Own Thinking Around Disability

When I arrived to teaching, having grown up in my predominantly white, middle-class community, I believed that my evaluation of the students' ability was objective and neutral. After all, I was trained as a technician in reading acquisition and phonetics-based approaches to learning. Following my degree in psychology and prior to completing my Bachelor of Education, I attended workshops and international professional development programs led by neurologists, educational psychologists, and renowned scientists and scholars. I was trained to spot deficits in language comprehension and how to clinically address them. I was shown images and videos of brain scans and understood their ability to detect the slightest degree of impairment, as they could when areas of the brain related to decoding and reading were implicated. I could speak to clients about neurofunction, synaptic pathways, and the malleability of the brain and its potential to rewire with the instructional treatment I was trained to offer. I was comfortable with my expertise and, as a young, white woman in the field of education, my expertise was rarely challenged.

Later, I left my community to pursue a degree in education. The program's tenets were steeped in equity and social justice, and I was lost. Not quite sure how or where I fit in the program, I submitted course papers disputing the idea that class or race discrimination could influence educators' notions of ability. I argued that the assessment tools used to identify deficits in language, reading, and comprehension were benign tools that offered objective truths.

I struggled to understand the complicated relationship between racism, classism, and schooling opportunities. While my colleagues were arguing about how race and class matters in approaches to education and learning, I, comfortable in all my clinical experience, argued that I was on the side of "science." At the time, it didn't matter to me who was assessed because I believed that impairment was objective, measurable, and real. To this point, my understanding of ability was a simple equation—identify impairment (physical, psychical, intellectual) and apply a treatment (medical intervention, therapy, training). In my opinion, involving context only risked muddying access to the treatments one needed and deserved. To me, the most equitable approach was to identify and fix.

When I began the Bachelor of Education program, I was surprised that others could hold such diverse perspectives on ability and could dismiss what I believed as foundational understandings around the identification and treatment of disability in schools. One of the course directors took particular issue with my positioning of disability. He was a longtime activist who had worked for decades addressing issues of poverty and education, particularly for immigrant and working-class families. Not only was he a prolific writer and editor, but he was also active in politics and committed to advocacy, working with and for historically marginalized families. We were born in the same city and had gone to the same university, yet we held notably divergent views. Generally, in the Bachelor of Education program, I did well on written assignments and the assignment on biases in education was no different. However, when it was time to hand back my work, my professor did not immediately let go of the paper. Instead, he held my work and my gaze and shared, "I gave you an A, because you argued it well, but know that I disagree with everything you've said." Once he let go, I rammed the paper into my bag, and smiled at my colleagues, but the exchange had rattled me. As the classroom was small and the entirety of my cohort had heard, now busily pretending they hadn't, it had been a very public rebuke. And rightfully so. Everything I had written was an offense to the communities he had dedicated his life to supporting. I had dismissed the possibilities of racial and class discrimination and injustice in terms of perceptions of ability. He had dedicated his life to working with families who had been disenfranchised through special education and streaming practices. Years later, I called him at his home to apologize and say he had been right about everything.

The year came when I decided to pursue a graduate program in critical disability studies which, with my experience in education, landed me in the field of DSE. Graduate studies allowed me to ask questions such as: How do schools respond to disability and what does that tell us about how ability is valued? What barriers are found within classes, schools, and systems as they relate to ability? What role do systems, such as special education or streaming, play in perpetuating a deficit understanding of disability? How, then, does our understanding of ability shape our decisions on how best to support children? Throughout my graduate studies, I was fortunate to land a position within our school district's research office. There, I could ask such questions of the system from a DSE perspective. Using district data, I could investigate how ability functions as an explicit organizational factor for schools as well as work with communities to imagine new possibilities.

Drawing on DSE literature and interviews with students, educators and administrators, this book explores how ability-based approaches to schooling negatively impact disability identity, create dangerous discourses around ability and notions of care, lead to disparate academic pathways and outcomes, and contribute to oppressive conditions for disabled youth. This book is organized into three parts: 1) the first part of the book (Chapters 1–3) examines how we think about ability, disability and ableism in schools; 2) the second part of the book (Chapters 4–6) explores how schools organize students by ability; and 3) the last part of the book (Chapters 7–8) examines strategies educators can implement in their practice to challenge ableism and support students. Throughout, I will delve into the theorization underlying DSE as well as explore and imagine what disability rights and justice could look like in schools.

Overview of the Book

The first chapter, "Making Disability a Different Kind of Issue in Schools: Disability Studies in Education," explores how and why it is important to think about disability from a social justice perspective. Disability studies in education (DSE) offers many tools to explore ability-based practices and their impact on students. Proponents of DSE argue that the way schools respond to disability is neither objective nor neutral and that ability-based decisions are often rooted in ableism. This chapter explores disability rights and justice frameworks that educators can use to think through their own practices.

How we think about ability is inherently tied to how we respond to it. Ability is not a single, measurable, static trait. The search for a singular measure of intelligence has been mired in racist, classist, and anti-immigration histories and ideologies. Chapter 2, "How Ability Is Constructed and Organized in Schools," explores the history of ability testing, different approaches and theories of developmentalism often taken up in education, and the impact of ability-based programs on students' experiences in school.

Special education and academic streaming have had a long and complicated relationship with gender, race, and class. Children who are racialized, who live in lower income families, identify as male, who are multilingual learners, or newly immigrated to North America are often overrepresented in special education and lower academic tracks. For example, when the special education population is broken down according to categories of exceptionality or disability, patterns suggest that racial, class, and other forms of bias may be shaping educators' perceptions of students' ability. Chapter 3, "Detangling the Relationship Between Race, Class, and Perceived Ability," discusses how ableism is inextricably linked to racism, classism, and other forms of bias circulating in schools and emphasizes the importance of viewing student ability through a critical lens.

When children are perceived as disabled, schools often turn to special education as a source of funding and support. But is it successful? Chapter 4, "Special Education Programs, Identification, and Placement," will review the practice and implications of moving students through the special education identification process and the assignment of special education placements, as well as explore the development and implementation of individualized education plans/programs (IEP).

There are many ways to organize children by ability in schools and these can change across elementary and secondary panels. While special education does exist at the secondary level, in high school, a new organizational system known as streaming (tracking), is introduced. In many districts, secondary students are organized across different academic streams. Each stream is intended to provide a modified program to support students' learning and prepare them for post–high school pursuits. But do they deliver? And for who? Chapter 5, "Academic Streaming and Hierarchies of Ability," will ask readers to think about why it is important to critically look at the similarities between systems, the shift in language and perspective, and what it might mean when it comes to justifying who eventually has the opportunity to graduate and access postsecondary education.

Up to this point, the book explores the ways children and youth are disadvantaged in schools through ability-based approaches to learning. However, we cannot push for disability rights or justice in schools unless we also challenge the ways in which ability is privileged and celebrated. Chapter 6 delves into the historical and current notions of giftedness and talent; it also explores the role that gifted and elite education play in exacerbating inequity in schools. Chapter 6, "Implicating Gifted and Talented Education," examines the role of programs for students deemed "talented" and explores how whiteness and wealth become integrated in notions of ability to further solidify privilege and exclusive programming.

After having examined the subjectivity of ability and its organizational role in schools, how can educators orient their practice to resist perpetuating ableism in their classrooms? Chapter 7, "Critical Approaches to Inclusion," provides an overview of what inclusion is and what it is not. This chapter explores different notions of and approaches to inclusion as well as describes the consequences of exclusionary practice from student perspectives. Chapter 7 also discusses how adopting a DSE framework can empower students, families, and educators.

Principles are important in guiding our practice—but it is also valuable to have some strategies that promotes inclusion. Chapter 8, "Inclusive Pedagogy and Practice," includes a number of practices that educators can use in their classrooms. These practices range from adopting culturally responsive and relevant pedagogy; differentiated and direct instruction; accommodations; developing class profiles, assessment, visual schedules; and other ideas to enhance accessibility and inclusion within the classroom.

Despite the overwhelming empirical evidence and feedback from youth, families, and educators, the debate around whether inclusive education is appropriate for disabled children continues to be taken up in the public realm. Some families and educators express genuine concern over students' welfare within general education. Others adamantly employ rights discourses to ensure that education systems maintain self-contained special education programs and tracking systems. The final chapter, "Moving Forward and Setting New Conditions for Justice," examines historical and current notions of inclusion, drawing on strategies equity-seeking groups have developed to counter racial, cultural, as well as gender and sexual discrimination. This chapter closes considering the possibilities for disability justice in schools.

The research included in this book is largely drawn from a Canadian context, specifically from Ontario, Canada's most populous province. Due to a number of similarities across systems, connections to US based practices and policies are discussed. In collaboration with district and academic researchers, I have worked with a number of public schools and school districts particularly on their approaches to special education and streaming to promote greater inclusion. Critical insights from over 85 interviews and focus-group participants are integrated into the themes of this book. I find that discussions on disability and schooling, particularly those concerning special education, rarely include disabled students' perspectives. But who would know the experience and impact of ability-grouping better? Through our research, youth articulated how their involvement in special education and/or lower tracked programs have led to stigma and bullying within the school; they have described how placement in special education and lower academic tracks have shaped their sense of self. Youth, educators, and administrators identified specific practices that they feel create barriers, particularly for communities that have experienced historical marginalization through racialization, poverty, immigration, and the like, and revealed strategies to support equity work in schools. Through our interviews, each group shared important insights into how educators and administrators can push for disability justice in their schools. As such, the chapters include recommendations on how educators can enact the principles described throughout the book and concludes with questions for further thought and reflection.

Ableism in Education

Rethinking School Practices
and Policies

Part I

Thinking Through Ability, Disability, and Ableism

1

Making Disability a Different Kind of Issue in Schools: Disability Studies in Education

"The phrase 'disabled people' does not treat disability as passive or an afterthought. Disability exists as a consequence of an active process of marginalization—people are disabled."
—WITHERS, 2012, P. 7

Ability and disability are complicated, but it can be helpful to consider them "simultaneously" (Goodley, 2014, p. xi). For many in education, the notion of ability is a linear one, where students' ability develops and is measured in relation to developmental and/or grade level expectations. In schools, ability is typically viewed as an asset ascribed to students who meet or exceed developmental or grade level expectations. Should students fail to meet these expectations, their perceived inability is often understood as a deficit, potentially triggering further assessments to uncover whether there could be underlying impairment.

But not everyone views ability as value added and disability as value diminished. Not everyone understands ability or disability the way it is typically discussed in schools, as something that can be captured or compartmentalized into Western and medicalized categories of impairment. Culturally, there are wide variations in how disability is understood, from divine intervention to social construction. Many Indigenous approaches to disability counter the idea of impairment and instead understand disability as a gift (Ineese-Nash et al., 2017; Lovern & Locust, 2013). For many disability advocates, disability is an identity that reflects experiences of disablement and links these experiences to a collective movement.

Most school districts ascribe to a fairly narrow understanding of disability, often tying disability to special education. For many students, the first time they or their families engage with assessment or identification processes might be through their school, creating a unique tension between how schools think about disability and how students understand themselves as disabled. Additionally, there are contextual influences where students only experience certain forms of ability or disability in relation to specific school activities, but not in other aspects of their lives. The key takeaway here is that when working with students and their families, how ability or disability is discussed in special education may be unfamiliar to or in conflict with families' own beliefs and standpoints.

First, a Quick Note on Language in This Text

As part of a larger political movement, many people within the disability community have called for a reclamation of the word *disabled* and a shift from person-first language (e.g., students with disabilities) to identity-first language (e.g., disabled students). As Annamma and Morrison (2018, endnote 5) describe, "…disability is an identity to be claimed, similar to race." This reorientation in language aligns with the more recent reclamations of identities such as *queer* in relation to sexuality and *mad* for those who identify as psychiatric survivors. For this text, I adopt identity-first terminology throughout this book to politically align with the disability rights and justice movements. Special education, as a system, can perpetuate exclusion and stigma for disabled students, particularly through its identification and referral practices, deficit-orientation, and academically limited and limiting programming. Therefore, unless reiterating direct quotes or variables used in research, I use the term *disabled students* in place of the oft-used term *students with special education needs*. Some may suggest that not all students identified with "special needs" have a formally recognized disability. However, I would argue that students identified with special needs frequently encounter disabling conditions in school in relation to their identification and subsequent label or placement, therefore, believe it to be an appropriate representation.

Language is important. I would be remiss to not also include my dislike for the terms *special education*, *special education needs*, and all disability-related idioms that attempt to erase the experience of disability. The term *special*, in relation to disability, attempts to hide disability stigma and discrimination behind a 'nicer' word, a patronizing word, like *special*. But we all know what special means, and the fact that education is not comfortable naming disability only adds to its otherness. Children certainly know what special means. I visit a lot of schools and the number of times I have heard kids snicker at each other "Oh, don't mind him, he's *special*," makes clear that this attempt to address disability stigma through scrubbing disability from education language has failed. Having said that, special education is the widely recognized name of the educational processes responsible for organizing, funding, and supporting disabled students in schools. It is inscribed in legislation, policy, and system data. Therefore, its usage in this text is sometimes inescapable.

Ability and Schooling

Ability is not only central to the purpose of schooling, but foundational to the way schools operate. After all, schooling is intended to build capacity. As mentioned in the introduction, children have the right to education, to go to school and learn new skills, new ways of thinking, and new understandings of the world. Through school, they learn how to develop and improve their ability to think critically and hone important skills. In school, children and youth learn how to exercise civic rights and responsibilities so they can participate to their fullest in broader society. Because learning and skill development are essential to schooling, students' ability and degree of mastery of skills are continuously assessed and measured to ensure both institutional and student-centered goals are being met.

Regardless of its central role in schools, ability is a much-discussed concept that is simultaneously difficult to define. A recent study showed that the very concept of ability can change dependent on whether educators are describing students struggling or excelling with achievement. For students who were perceived to struggle, ability was understood more often as something fixed or static, yet for students who were doing well in school, ability was often seen as something malleable, responsive, and indicative of potential (Ladwig & McPherson, 2017). As such, researchers concluded that one of the primary ways ability was typically used in schools was to rank and organize students and justify the learning opportunities they were subsequently offered (Ladwig & McPherson, 2017).

Messages solidifying the relationship between ability and hierarchical ranking of students in schools can be circulated and promoted unintentionally. However, intentional or not, these messages can have dramatic effects on students' sense of place and value within the school. For example, hierarchies based on ability can be established through simple practices such as rewarding students who are first to complete a task by also allowing them to be first out for recess, while students who take more time end up missing out on the opportunity to play or socialize. Students who demonstrate aptitude in reading are often grouped together and encouraged to pursue books that are more complex and interesting, while others are relegated to reading books below their age-level's interest. From this activity alone, all students involved know where they fall along the classroom's hierarchy of ability.

Once, while volunteering in a Grade 1 reading program, I sat with the "bluebirds," the reading group assigned slightly lower-than-grade-level material. Together, we were working through the phonetic structure of new words. But I couldn't help but notice that when distracted, most of my group were sneaking peeks at what the "robins" were doing. The robins were reading novels and working through a different kind of activity book. Near the end of our twenty minutes together, one exasperated bluebird shared that their goal for Grade 1 was to end the year as a robin so they could get to read the fun books. But at least, according to this one bluebird, they were somewhat lucky that they didn't have to read the same books as the "finches" because those were for "babies." Regardless of the unassuming avian-inspired names, each student in that classroom was keenly aware of where they fit within their class' ability hierarchy and equated higher-ability as "better."

There are many ways that ability hierarchies are reinforced in class-rooms and schools. Classroom representatives at school assemblies or events are typically selected from among higher achieving students. Hierarchies of ability can form when educators ask students to form groups to work on projects, but do not mitigate the dynamics that occur when students are not selected based on their academic perfor-mance. All of these practices are normalized in classrooms, but they still unintentionally establish who is perceived as able, unable, or dis-abled, and worse, model how students should expect to be rewarded or excluded based on their ability to perform.

Current Context of Special Education and Streaming

Special education and academic streaming (or *tracking* as it is referred to in the United States) are two of the most prominent ability-based strat-egies public schools use to organize student learning. They are often discussed as distinct systems, although both are anchored in ableist assumptions. Special education is considered to largely work with and for students identified as disabled or as having 'special education needs'. Academic streaming is more likely to be discussed as a consequence for poor performance, work ethic, or competency toward academics, in general. However, both systems use similar underlying notions of abil-ity, inability, and disability to drive decisions around organization and programming for students (e.g., gifted, talented, and elite education; trades and apprenticeship education, etc.). How systems understand ability determines who and what constitutes as able and deserving of future academic and career opportunities.

When we think about disability in schools, we often think about special education—and, as noted earlier, special education has a very specific way of thinking about disability. Generally, special education adopts a deficit view of disability, meaning disability is approached as something to be identified and fixed (Brantlinger, 2006). Special education functions on a premise that there is a normative way of being, learning, and behaving. As such, the special education system is tasked with addressing students whose being, learning, or behavior is believed to fall outside of this normative framework. Special education assumes that the identification of ability and normalcy can be objectively determined, devoid of context. But nothing could be further from the truth. *Normal* is contextually defined and often includes characteristics shaped by those in positions of power (Davis, 2013). Therefore, many communities who have faced historical marginalization correctly argue their children are often constructed or misidentified as falling outside a Western, Eurocentric and middle-class notion of the 'norm' and, as a result, are overrepresented within special education identifications and programs. This is particularly true for lower income, racialized, and some immigrant communities (Artiles et al., 2010; Reid & Knight, 2006).

For generations, special education has been the primary source of disability funding and support in public school systems across North America (Danforth et al., 2006). Anyone who has spent time in a public education system either as a student or staff likely has some familiarity with special education. They or their peers may have had access to special education resources or participated in special education programs. Special education is intended to provide students with an array of services including academic supports, individual education plans (IEP), accommodations, curricular modifications, and, in some school systems, alternative program placements. However, there is growing concern around how special education aligns with socially-just approaches to disability. In fact, I would argue that special education contributes to the confusion over social justice, equity, and disability in schools. I am frequently reminded that schools have established an entire system designed to meet the needs of disabled students. Is that not justice? If students are being supported through appropriate accommodations and modifications, what more could/should schools be doing?

But there is more to addressing disability discrimination than the provision of services and accommodations. Through special education's expansive reach, generations of students have come to further understand disability as impairment, thus influencing students' sense of self both within and outside of the special education system. Special education positions disability as an unfavorable difference and as an individual quality that needs to be remediated through specialized attention and instruction. And, typically, this difference is shrouded in secrecy, only furthering suspicion and stigma. For example, when students are pulled from class to attend special education, remaining students could be left with the impression that there might be, or must be, something different or *wrong* with their peers; something so significant that it could not be addressed in the classroom. From our work with students, many shared that they were never told why they were pulled from class for special education support. To them it was a mystery. However, they were keenly aware that their peers held suspicions and thought differently of them because of it. The prolific understanding of disability as deficit, invisibilized, and subsequently shamed, is perpetuated through special education and is exactly why we need a reorientation of what disability means and what disability justice could look like in schools.

Social Justice and Disability

Social justice and equity discourses have long been integrated into education discussions, core tenets of professional development sessions for educators, and within popular approaches to pedagogical and curriculum studies. But when it comes to education more broadly, the overuse of the terms *social justice* and *equity* has caused them to lose their edge. Instead, these terms have been adopted into policy documents with vacuous aims and unclear principles intended to encompass all forms of inequity, but, in practice, addressing nothing. The disability rights movements, in both the United States and Canada, have paved the way for substantive changes to policy and legislation, promoting the rights of disabled Americans and Canadians. But access to rights frameworks can be restrictive and can privilege those in a position to wield other forms of power or influence.

As such, rights, alone, is insufficient. Yes, more than ever, disabled people are winning court cases and human rights claims. The rights to inclusion, to housing, and to employment are increasingly recognized through the lens of discrimination. But the work is slow and results tend not to reflect the experiences of the disabled community as a whole. As having signed and ratified the Conventions on the Rights of Persons with Disabilities (CRPD) (United Nations, 2006), in Canada, the rights to receive care at home, to self-determination and independence, and even the right to life are enshrined. Yet for many, particularly those facing multiple and intersecting forms of oppression, through racial, economic, sexual, and anti-immigration discrimination, these are not a reality. Note that as of this writing, the United States has signed the CRPD but it has not yet been ratified.

COVID-19 has shone a light on the systemic abuses that disabled people are expected to endure on a regular basis. As COVID-19 ripped through long-term care facilities and group homes, the apathy toward the massive loss of disabled lives was astounding. The inaccurate rhetoric around "don't worry, only people with underlying conditions are vulnerable to this virus" (Parekh & Underwood, 2020) was a direct devaluation of the lives of disabled people. The politicization of protecting others (e.g., mask wearing, vaccinating, adhering to public health restrictions) in the United States, and to a lesser extent in Canada, led to innumerable deaths of those who did not choose to obfuscate the recommendations. Close to 70% of COVID-19 related deaths in Canada were long-term care residents as compared to the international average of 41% for that sector (Ireton, 2021). While many long-term care residents died from COVID-19, several others died of neglect (Stevenson, 2021). While we may think of long-term care residents as solely elderly, note that every resident in long-term care is there because they are disabled. Access to equitable health care, education, and support services continues to be fraught with barriers. After years of advocacy, activism, and ongoing work by the disability community, shifting institutional values and cultures remains an ever-present and urgent priority.

Disability Theory and Disability Movements

In order to affect change, educators concerned with how ability and disability are taken up in schools should first grapple with the core institutional values and cultures that shape their work. In this regard, theory can be really helpful in making sense of the education system, as well as guide educators as to how best to address injustice. Disability studies in education (DSE) adopts critical disability theory and applies it to the field of education and schooling. Ability-related oppression in schools can take on many forms, including ableism, disablism, structural ableism, and sanism. As such, disability advocates and activists have forwarded frameworks centering disability justice, noting its interconnectedness with other justice-seeking movements.

Disability Studies in Education

DSE is a growing field of study that uses critical disability theory to examine education-related practices, structures, and student outcomes. Critical disability theory explores how disability is constructed and understood in relation to political, economic, social, historical and environmental factors. As such, DSE resists narrow and medically-oriented interpretations of disability and, instead, investigates how the conditions in schools can enable or disable students' participation, achievement, and sense of belonging or value. Like critical disability studies, DSE is rooted in activism and advocacy. DSE principles propose new ways to think about the relationship between disability, educational practices, and social justice. Critical disability studies is interdisciplinary by nature and does not typically ascribe to disability as an isolated or singular issue. Therefore, critical disability theory often explores how disability is understood in relation to other theoretical frameworks such as critical race and feminist studies, historical materialism, and sociology. As a result of its interdisciplinary nature, DSE is an ideal approach to use when reenvisioning education and schooling, and how best to support disabled students.

DSE provides an opportunity to think through the politics of disability—both in its enactment and identity—as they play out in schools; a markedly different approach to disability than what has been historically practiced in public or special education. As such, educators using a DSE framework in their work may encounter initial pushback, particularly as they attempt to challenge well-established institutional values that are rooted in ableism. DSE, along with disability justice movements, highlight the interconnectedness between myriad forms of oppression. For example, DSE highlights how ableism has the potential to harm all students, not just disabled students. DSE discusses how ableism can be used in schools to enact other forms of discrimination, such as racism and classism. As such, DSE can be a powerful tool, enabling families and educators to challenge unjust practices in schools. As awareness grows, there are increasingly more education resources delving into anti-oppressive approaches to schooling that adopt a DSE approach (Baglieri & Lalvani, 2020; Cosier & Ashby, 2016; Lawrence-Brown & Sapon-Shevin, 2014).

Thinking Through Ableism, Disablism, and Sanism in the Context of Schools

When ability is the key organizational factor in schools, ableism poses a significant danger. In short, ableism is a form of discrimination based on real or perceived ability (Hall, 2019). Ableism is essentially the privileging of ability that conditionally aligns human value to perceived ability, consequently devaluing disability and disabled people. Ableism is not only experienced by students but is also imposed on them by the institutional values and priorities of schooling. Depending on where you live, you may be more familiar with the terms *ableism* or *disablism* to describe the oppression and discrimination disabled people face. For example, in North America the term *ableism* is more frequently used, whereas in Europe, *disablism* is more popular. In many cases, these terms are used interchangeably (Chapman & Withers, 2019). However, Goodley (2014) provides a clearer distinction between the two terms. *Ableism* sets the standard by which others are measured. Ableism privileges independence, measurable achievement, the ability to work and contribute to the economy. "Ableism breeds paranoia, confusion, fear and inadequacy. Ableism is an ideal that no one ever matches up to" (Goodley, 2014, p. xi).

Ableism drives notions of meritocracy and is interwoven into the very fabric of schools and the principles of contemporary schooling. As Goodley (2014) notes, ableism is what shapes our fears of not measuring up, not fitting in, of not being good or worthy or successful enough to be included or belong in community with others. In schools, ableism rewards ability and offers students more interesting, stimulating, and worthwhile opportunities based on their demonstration of ability. Ableism is the promotion of ability-based competition. Ableism is the privileging of elite, ability-based programs over general programs or support-focused programs. Ableism is the practice of putting the most-skilled educators in classrooms with the most-skilled students. In schools, ableism could be embedded within nonreflexive and rigid measures of academic achievement.

In Goodley's (2014) interpretation, disablism is more overt discrimination towards disability and "relates to the oppressive practices of contemporary society that threaten to exclude, eradicate and neutralize those individuals, bodies, minds and community practices that fail to fit the capitalist imperative" (p. xi). In schools, disablism can be identified through the practices that result in the exclusion of disabled students. For example, the practice of removing disabled students from the classroom because they are deemed unfit to learn with their peers. Denying access to quality education programs and relevant and responsive curriculum as well as denying access to accommodations within the school are other examples of disablism. Disablism is integrated into the practice of segregated bussing and segregated school entrances. Orchestrated exclusion takes many forms: removing students' right to go to recess or to join peers for lunch, forcing children to go to "quiet" rooms or asking families to keep their children home from school as a result of their impairment. As Goodley notes, disablism "is a powerful narrative that guides the politics of disabled people's movements and politicizes the experience of life in a disabled world" (2014, p. xi). Like ableism, disablism is political and demands a political response. To ensure work is equity-centered, educators must challenge such practices and draw attention to policies that result in exclusion.

Another form of ability-based discrimination is sanism. *Sanism* specifically refers to the oppression and denial of rights in response to those with histories of mental illness (Poole et al., 2012). The concept of sanism has been an integral part of Mad Studies. An offshoot of critical disability studies, Mad Studies focuses on the experiences and advocacy of psychiatrized patients and psychiatric survivors, and of those who identify as "mad" (Poole et al., 2012). Just as critical disability studies challenges the medicalization and pathologization of disability, Mad Studies challenges the psychiatrization of Mad people and the prevalence of sanism within the politics and practices of care. In schools, sanism can be exemplified through lowered expectations for students, withholding accommodations, denying students opportunities for self-care, and the use of popularized sanist language like "don't be crazy" or "that's so insane."

This is important for schools. My colleague, Dr. Robert S. Brown, and I just completed a study on whether students self-identified as having a disability (see Parekh & Brown, 2020). We then compared the rates of self-identification alongside the rates of institutional identification (or the identifications provided through special education). Interestingly, there were many students who self-identified as disabled, but were not institutionally identified through special education. We query the extent to which these students were reporting disability due to mental illness as mental illness and/or mental health-related disabilities are one of the most prevalent conditions experienced by youth (Chatoor, 2021).

Critically important in the context of schooling, *structural ableism* describes how ableism can be mediated by and embedded within systems. Structural ableism creates ability-based hierarchies as well as produces disparities in access and resources (Dolmage, 2017). Structural ableism can be enacted through policy, legacy practices, or curriculum that reflect the cultural values of the school or system. In fact, I would argue that structural ableism is a key factor in the enactment of many forms of discrimination, such as racism and classism, in schools (more on this in Chapter 3). For example, many critical scholars examine the relationship between notions of ability and whiteness (Gaztambide-Fernández et al., 2013; Leonardo & Broderick, 2011) and study the relationship between wealth and perceptions of talent (Gaztambide-Fernández & Parekh, 2017) that are then structurally reinforced through schooling practices. While ableism is the privileging of ability, it is important to reflect on how biased notions of ability are further formalized through educational structures such as program and placement.

Disability Justice

Disability justice provides a comprehensive framework which examines the multiple oppressions that collude to enact disablement. Forged by disabled activists, namely queer activists of color, a movement toward disability justice sought to center the experiences of disabled people often erased by the disability rights movement (Berne, 2015). As noted, the disability rights movement and disability studies have historically privileged the experiences of white disabled activists and scholars, often ignoring the multifaceted forms of oppression and intersections of identity that shape the experiences of disability and disablement.

Among other core tenets, disability justice demands that activists and allies deeply engage with intersectionality, commit to economic justice and collective liberation (Berne, 2015). The important message being that disability justice cannot be achieved in isolation from other justice-seeking movements, just as disability cannot be addressed as an isolated issue or experience. Likewise, disability justice cannot be achieved without radical and systemic changes to the institutions that continue to construct disability and produce the conditions for economic, social, and political disablement.

DSE often regards inclusive education as a preferred alternative to a special education model of support. However, inclusion alone is not justice. Disability justice requires the active dismantling of all exclusionary processes and practices that have been continuing unabated for generations across US and Canadian public schools. We need a reimagining of what pedagogical practice looks like in the classroom, as well as a restructuring of how we allocate and align support for students. But even as there is much work to be done in education, our work includes building partnerships with families and educators as well as committing to reorientating the core values and cultural practice in schools that perpetuate ableism (see Hatt, 2012).

To promote disability justice in schools, it's important to push institutions, primarily public education systems, to engage more critically with how the construction of ability and ableism influences students in the immediate and long term. I believe education matters and that it significantly shapes the life courses of youths. I also believe there is a hesitancy in education to name the role ability and ableism play within its deepest core. I believe schools hold potential to affect change—and change is desperately needed. The timing feels urgent, and to really address the issue of ableism in schools, disability justice must be the way forward.

Strategies to Begin the Work of Addressing Systemic Ableism in Schools

In relation to our current public education systems, integrating a DSE approach may sound like a lot of undoing of historical practices—and it is. However, examining disability through a DSE lens also enables and encourages opportunities for innovation in education. Here are a few ideas that may help advance disability justice in schools.

Classroom

At the classroom level, integrating a DSE approach may mean rethinking assessment, what we assess, and how we conduct assessment. When developing assessment, it is helpful to consider the alternate forms in which we will accept the demonstration of knowledge or mastery. Resisting the practice of grouping students by ability and untethering privileges or advantages to academic performance are important strategies to address ableism in the classroom. Of course we want to encourage academic achievement, but tying rewards—such as extra time at recess, getting first pick of activities, getting to be the classroom leader—to academic performance will inadvertently establish a hierarchy in which some children will be consistently left behind.

Intentional intervention in social dynamics is important. If you observe mocking, exclusion, or suspect bullying to be occurring, intervene; identify and name it. Intentionally establish classroom values that extend beyond academic achievement and ensure that these values are inclusive of and cocreated with your students. Talk with students. What can we learn from their experiences in the classroom? Normalize students expressing their needs to you and others, not just academic needs. Help identify how you and all students can support the class. Intentionally describe and model the various ways students can support their classmates and foster community. Also, model the importance of interdependency and how each student brings gifts and contributes to the classrooms in valuable ways. More on this in Chapters 7 and 8 when discussing approaches and strategies for inclusion.

School

Using DSE to examine the structure of a school can be immensely helpful in identifying ableism and ways to intervene. Reviewing *how* students access support can help uncover whether or how ability may be a central organizational factor within the school. For example, do students have access to support within the classroom? Are they pulled out of the classroom for resource? Are they placed in a separate special education class? How might these various approaches support and value students as members of a classroom or school community? How might these approaches create or reinforce a hierarchy within a school? How might the use of space and location of support influence the role students play in the social fabric of the school? At the school level, DSE principles ask us to reflect on the language we use, how we describe students to others, and what decisions we make in relation to our understanding of student ability. DSE principles also ask us to think about how other forms of discrimination are implicated in decisions that are seemingly ability-based; they urge us to cultivate new ideas on how to support students and create successful learning environments.

Within a school, educators may have to make decisions concerning which students are referred to special education or which students will be streamed into non-Academic programming. But how are these decisions informed? What knowledge, impressions, perceptions, and understandings of the student are we drawing on? Professional development to raise awareness around ableism can be useful, but establishing an anti-ableist culture within the school is likely even more effective. It is important for educators and administrators within the school to review how students and programs are celebrated and profiled. For schools that host a diversity of ability-based or specialized programs (e.g., elite arts/sports programs), this can be a particular challenge.

To begin implementing system change at the school level, I advise starting with schools who volunteer. Begin with educators who share a commitment to justice and are keen to forge a new learning environment and approach. Staff classrooms with educators who are committed to challenging ableism and who support inclusion, so students identified through special education or who have a history of streaming are supported within the classroom. Ensure that the learning spaces that are intentionally working to address ableism and inclusion are open and can function as demonstration classrooms within the school. Strategically schedule timetables to enable opportunities for educators to coplan and coteach. Coteaching can dramatically reduce the need for pullout services for students and can seamlessly integrate support so that all students in the classroom benefit, not only those formally identified as requiring special education.

District Level

It is important that districts articulate their commitment to disability justice and address its integral relationship with the aims of equity-seeking groups. Challenge implicit and explicit forms of ability-grouping whether that be through the expansion of self-contained programming or lower academic streaming. Not only have these strategies been shown to improve academic performance but they have also been identified as key strategies to reduce racial and class inequality (Archer et al., 2018; Hehir et al., 2016; Lavrijsen & Nicaise, 2015; Matthewes, 2018; Rubin, 2006). Communication with families is critical and district communication must reassure families that movements toward greater inclusion are in the best interest of students. Schools that have experienced success in establishing more inclusive approaches to education should be profiled and made accessible to communities of educators seeking guidance on implementation. Resources should be distributed through the system to enable professional development and engagement with successful learning models.

All of these strategies require a reorientation in how ability and disability are typically understood and responded to in schools. But all are possible.

Questions for Further Thought and Reflection

1. In your school, what kind of language or words are used to describe disability? What images do they illicit? Are they rooted

in deficit thinking or do they speak to the social experience of disability? Are they honoring of students?

2. Does your school offer ability-based programs (e.g., self-contained special education programs, programs geared toward students identified as gifted or talented)? If so, do you notice a difference in how these programs are viewed within and outside the school? How are these programs prioritized in terms of resource allocation within the school or district? Should disparities exist, how might they impact the self-conceptualization of the students within those programs?

3. If your school offers resource, special education, or ability-based programming, where are these programs located within the school? Are they close to the main office, in a separate wing, close to certain other programs or resources within the school? What might be the rationale for their location? How might the location of these programs enable access or create barriers for student participation within the school community?

2

How Ability Is Constructed and Organized in Schools

"Of all the tyrannies a tyranny sincerely exercised for the good of its victims may be the most oppressive."
—C. S. LEWIS (AS CITED IN DINEEN, 1996, p. 15)

We all make assumptions as to what ability looks like in our own daily lives. We may recognize ability in our work, in our families, and in our own activities. As educators, we are required to use our professional judgment to identify when students are struggling and to help them navigate through school and engage with the curriculum in a way that enhances their learning. Teacher education programs provide guidance on assessment, particularly in relation to specific curricular subjects or particular learning processes; but educators must also rely on more implicit assessment to monitor student progress in certain skill areas, such as executive functioning, organization, self-regulation, and so forth.

I have taught in teacher education programs at different institutions and my classes largely address issues related to special education, disability, and inclusion. Regularly, teacher candidates approach me with questions directly about students they have observed in their placements. Many of these concerns, stemming from genuine care, begin similarly to this: "I have this student in my class and there's clearly 'something going on' or 'something wrong.' They do not have an individual education plan, but there is some kind of disability there that I think needs to be addressed. What should I do?" Following this kind of query, the pre-candidate teacher would often provide an overview of the things the school-age student could not do or would detail how they failed to perform in the classroom as expected. In response, I would often begin by asking how they knew there was something going on with this particular student, what kinds of assessments they or the classroom teacher conducted, and what information they used to inform their perception. Often, I would be met with the response, "Well, I can just tell."

The assumption that, as educators, we can *just tell* when something is *wrong* with a child is possibly the most unexamined and dangerous assumption made within public education. In most cases, when teacher candidates raise concerns over a particular student's ability or achievement within the classroom, they are doing exactly what educators are expected to do. Educators are expected to use their judgment to discern when and how a student may be struggling, and they are expected to intervene. Educators are asked to use this judgment to help them figure out which assessments, resources, and accommodations may be necessary to support students in their classroom. But this place of discernment is rarely examined. When educators interpret what they observe in the classroom, personal contexts, worldviews, and positionalities can play a significant role. Teacher education programs can help develop skills and approaches to assessment, but, in many cases, we practice what we know. If we have been schooled in whiteness (Castagno, 2014) and medicalized/individualized notions of ability then our practice could be influenced by deficit understandings of ability that disproportionately impact racialized communities. For many of us, this is what has been done unto us, and unless intentionally interrupted, there's a good chance we will continue to do unto others.

It is imperative that educators identify and address how best to support students, but far too often what is observed in the classroom—whether it be related to students' behavior, attention, or skills—is interpreted as disorder, pathology, or impairment. In our work, educators are asked to navigate assumptions about student ability all the time. As such, critical reflective practice is important. Also important is recognizing how public education has ascribed to beliefs and practices that explicitly limit educators' ability to approach a child's learning holistically and embrace inclusive practice. For instance, the beliefs that, (1) psychometric testing reveals a "truth" about a child and informs educators how best to teach; (2) child development occurs in a linear way and reaching developmental milestones can be evaluated in isolation; (3) ability-grouping works and offers students, particularly lower achieving students, enhanced access to both their teacher and the curriculum.

The Murky History of Ability Testing

Psychometric testing for intelligence is a common assessment strategy in special education practice. Many special education identifications use psychometric evidence of cognitive impairment or exceptionality as part of their criteria. Testing results can also weigh heavily into the types of strategies implemented to support students whether that be support in the classroom or placement in a special education program. In many cases, testing can be arranged by a child's school, but families can also seek out independent psychometric testing, often at considerable expense.

Ability testing and the notion of intelligence was historically premised on the idea that intelligence was largely genetically derived (Ladwig & McPherson, 2017). Biological determinism suggests that our hereditary and genetic makeup—our biology—are solely or largely responsible for our behavior and social structures (Ryan, 2000; Sloan, 2013). Although debunked, biological determinism led researchers to think that "intelligence is genetically-based and permanently fixed . . . " (Sloan, 2013, para. 6). Despite a push to expand notions of ability in the field of education, "the dominant views of ability that circulate in schools have not broken free of the historical views of intelligence based on biology and heredity, at least in the Northern hemisphere" (Ladwig & McPherson, 2017, p. 346).

In the late 1800s, Galton developed the term *eugenics* and worked with statistical theory to help develop the concept of the *norm* (Davis, 2013). The consequences of applying the notion of a norm onto human bodies and human qualities is that it leads to assumptions around deviance. As Davis stated, "The new ideal of ranked order is powered by the imperative of the norm, and then is supplemented by the notion of progress, human perfectibility, and the elimination of deviance, to create a dominating, hegemonic vision of what the human body should be" (Davis, 2013, p. 5). What Davis was saying is that once we have adopted a need to meet the norm, we have created characteristics and bodies that are both idealized or devalued.

The belief that biology alone was responsible for the expression of ability, as well as linked to poverty and criminality, led to disastrous abuses of disabled people. In 1927, a statement from the United States Supreme Court read, "it is better for all the world if, instead of waiting to execute degenerate offspring for crime, or to let them starve for their imbecility, society can prevent those who are manifestly unfit from continuing their kind" (Bowal & Pecson, 2011, p. 49). While the constructed relationship between criminality and disability and the Court's definition of fitness are highly problematic, this position was not unusual for its time and was echoed through sterilization policies in both the United States and Canada.

In his text, Gould (1996) identified a series of historical practices in the field of psychology, such as a craniometry and other approaches used to measure intelligence, which have since been debunked, and raised concerns about the ongoing practice of intelligence testing. Tracing the development of eugenic theory through Galton's *Hereditary Genius* (1869) to the co-opting of Binet and Simon's Binet-Simon Intelligence Scale (1905) (Feldman & Sutcliffe, 2009), to Terman's 1916 version of the Intelligence Quotient (IQ) test, the Stanford-Binet Intelligence Scale (Gibbons & Warne, 2019) reveals a historical understanding of ability as biologically determined and manifested as a measurable characteristic. Terman's own writings revealed his support of biological determinism as a primary cause of observed differences in intelligence testing scores across racial identities and class statuses (Terman, 1916). He supported a eugenic and segregationist agenda that was used to justify unspeakable violence on persons "failing" to score within a contrived notion of "average." (More on Terman and his influence on the study of giftedness in Chapter 6). The history of disabled people reveals the devastating consequences of tying notions of capacity to human value—some which led to a denial of rights, forced sterilization (see

Fagan, 2013 re: Leilani Muir sterilization case), and systematic murder of those deemed disabled or to have "low" intelligence, as through the Nazi euthanasia program (Aktion T4) (Ben-Moshe et al., 2014; United States Holocaust Memorial Museum, 2020).

Two cases highlight how intelligence testing was weaponized and used to devastate the lives of many. In the early 1900s, there was a trifecta of disability injustices occurring simultaneously: (1) mass institutionalization of disabled people (Braddock & Parish, 2001); (2) nonconsensual sterilization practices (Tilley et al., 2012); and (3) widespread use of intelligence testing to determine eligibility for both practices. Leilani Muir, from Alberta, and Carrie Buck, from Virginia, shared strikingly similar histories (see Malcomson, 2008). Both were committed by their caregivers and subsequently institutionalized as youth in facilities for persons with intellectual disabilities. Following their institutionalization, they underwent IQ testing and both tested in the "moron" category (using the technical terminology of the day) (See Malcomson, 2008; Wahlsten, 1997). Both jurisdictions had legislation that allowed the forced sterilization of those who, through IQ testing, were deemed as a "mental defective" (DenHoed, 2016; Malcomson, 2008; Mutcherson, 2017). As such, both young women were sterilized to ensure they could no longer procreate and pass along, what was assumed, to be deviant genetic dispositions to their children.

Following their institutionalization and sterilization, both women were eventually released and went on to marry. Later, Leilani Muir underwent subsequent intelligence testing only to result in "normative" scores (Ellwand, n.d.). Similarly, later in her life, Carrie Buck was also believed to be of "normative intelligence" (Gould, 1984). It is important to note, the later determination of normative intelligence for both women do not worsen the crime committed through forced sterilization. Nonconsensual sterilization is violence. But what these similar case studies highlight is that the violence inflicted upon institutionalized peoples was often justified by the use of psychometric testing—a tool, by all intents and purposes, which failed in either its implementation or in its assumptions (or both).

By the 1960s, as Kendi (2019) describes, "genetic explanations—if not the tests and the achievement gap itself—had largely been discredited"

(p. 102). Yet schools continue to use versions of these tests to inform special education decisions. Reported IQ remains a key criterion for certain special education categories and can play a significant role in determining student placement in special education programs.

Historically, the development and promotion of intelligence testing was not neutral. For instance, in many cases, it is unclear how assessment developers norm their results and account for sample recruitment and participation. Connor (2017) argues that many assessments have been normed on the experiences of white, middle-class children resulting in lower scores for racialized children and those from lower income homes. Therefore, it is not surprising that intelligence testing continues to play an integral role in practices that produce and maintain social, academic, and economic inequality across racial, class, and ability identities.

Regardless of its murky history, intelligence tests continue to be framed as having the capacity to unlock key information about our children we could not otherwise identify or understand. Despite a lack of consensus among researchers as to what intelligence is or means, some psychometric assessments are believed to "measure" intelligence like "a tape measure provides for height" (Sloan, 2013, para. 11). Considering its history, its implications in some of society's most violent chapters, and the ongoing critique of racial, cultural, and class bias, education's continued allegiance to IQ tests, particularly in today's special education practices, is puzzling.

So long as intelligence testing continues to play a major role in special education practices and hold supremacy over relational methods of assessment, it will continue to present as a major barrier in advancing disability justice. Following an extensive systematic review on education selection and notions of intelligence, researchers concluded, "The unquestioned belief in and value placed upon notions of intelligence would seem to be at the heart of how it influences people's sense of self and their social relations and consequently the life chances and educational practices they experience" (Rix & Ingham, 2021, p. 8). It is important that educators understand the limitations of psychometric testing, particularly its conclusions on students' capacity for learning. Regardless of what an intelligence test purports, classroom practices are most effective when they are developed in relationship with students.

Some Strategies to Counter the Oppressive Effects of Ability Testing

As much as one may resist, psychoeducational testing is not leaving education anytime soon. As Brantlinger (2006) noted, IQ testing is big business, and if districts can be convinced that such tests are integral to students' achievement, referrals for more testing will continue. Another complicating factor is that, quite often, based on the requirements of districts, students' and families' access to resources can be dependent on the results of psychoeducational tests. For that reason, even if families do not ascribe to the way psychoeducational assessments construct ability, nor believe in the aims of psychoeducational testing, many must comply in order to access critical resources to support their child. Therefore, as critical educators, we must envision ways to promote a more holistic and relational view of our students even when having to simultaneously incorporate reductive measures.

It is important to contextualize assessment results, recognizing their inherent bias and the flawed design of the measure (e.g., taking into account test anxiety, situational/environmental barriers at testing site, language, and cultural bias). The most important strategy in understanding how best to plan and support students in the classroom is to simply get to know them. In this regard, classroom-based assessment is critical—not necessarily an assessment of what students know or have learned, but assessment to learn whether the pedagogical approaches being used in the classroom are, themselves, successful. For instance, and this has happened on more than one occasion, I believe I have developed an interesting, exciting, and intricate series of lesson plans. However, when I later assess students' understanding of the material, results reveal suboptimal outcomes. So I have a choice to make: to conclude that the students were incapable of understanding the content, or conclude that the way I had attempted to teach that content was not successful. In such cases, I would likely reorient my approach and assess students again. It also does not hurt to ask students what strategies they find effective. If midway through a lesson you get the sense students are getting restless, losing focus, it's ok to stop and ask them what they think needs to change to make the lesson more interesting/engaging or to just abandon the lesson all together and go back to the drawing board. It's ok to reorient your approach, to make mistakes, and learn from them; seeing you model vulnerability allows students to take the same risks in their own work.

When you develop an understanding of what strategies work best for which students, your overall classroom approach can be developed to include aspects of each of these strategies. Chances are that the strategies you believe work best to accommodate certain students are strategies that will likely benefit and increase engagement for all students. Figuring out what works best for students in a classroom context cannot be based solely on the results of psychoeducational assessment. To be effective, educators must commit to differentiating and adapting their pedagogical strategies to best address how students learn.

The Myth of Meritocracy and Its Ties to Developmentalism

Competition built on meritocracy and historical notions of cognitive development also stymy the promotion of disability justice in schools. When you ask your friends or colleagues about their school experience, a typical response might be "I was a pretty good student," "I liked school, I did ok," or perhaps, "School wasn't for me. I didn't do that well." Typically, when asked, respondents often reflect on how they stacked up compared to their classmates and to the expectations of the school. In these reflections, there is generally an implicit reference as to how their ability was defined through their schooling experiences and how that notion of 'measuring up' lasted with them well into adulthood. Schools have long been considered society's primary sorting mechanism, particularly in relation to future access to postsecondary and labor-market opportunities

(Bourdieu, 1973). Since public schooling is largely based on merito-cratic values and practices, throughout their time in school, students develop a certain sense of competency (or lack thereof) in a variety of skills that later justifies their economic position in the workplace (Duncan-Andrade & Morrell, 2008). In other words, when future students find themselves in precarious or low-wage jobs, or conversely in permanent, well-paid positions, they might reflect back to their experience in school and think, well, this is what I deserve (Duncan-Andrade & Morrell, 2008).

As in schooling, ability is a central feature of meritocracy and can be the determining factor in who warrants status and rewards. In fact, scholars who initially worked with the social model of disability argued that the conditions of labor and shifting means of production significantly contributed to the construction of disability (Oliver, 1990). As production required more skilled labor and the conditions demanded greater efficiency and competition, more people were excluded from the work force and constructed as disabled (Gleeson, 1997; Gleeson, 1999). Similarly, in neoliberal societies, frameworks of meritocracy amplify which skills, abilities, and social connections are valued; not surprisingly, these are found to be largely in line with market values. Meritocracy is deeply ingrained in our social conscious, so much so that many believe ability-based hierarchies that privilege market values are entirely appropriate, and may not consider how ability itself is a social construct and highly susceptible to bias. When schooling practices follow meritocratic principles, the concept of ability as a construct often becomes obscured by the implementation of seemingly, objective ability-based measures.

If you have ever taken postsecondary courses in the fields of education, social work, psychology, or nursing, or have parented a child, you have likely been exposed to the concepts of developmentalism. Theories of developmentalism eschewed by developmental psychology suggest that the nature of children and the experience of childhood "are shaped primarily by their physical, psychological and emotional development" (James & James, 2012, para. 1). Once children enter school, the integral role their families, their cultural experiences, and historical contexts once played are likely to be replaced by highly individualistic and linear notions of development. In school, grades are generally linked to children's chronological ages and curriculum expectations are aligned with largely linear learning expectations. Much of the reading material found in schools is leveled, implicitly or explicitly intended to indicate children's development in literacy. Behavior management protocols are also developmentally informed.

There are many popular books that examine child development. Many such books come complete with developmental charts and projections upon which you can track your child's physical, intellectual, and behavioral development. For example, you might read that by 5 months of age most children are beginning to recognize their name, demonstrate strong head control, and can push themselves up from the floor, as well as babble incessantly (Mazel, 2020a). By 1 year, most children are standing on their own, saying names for parents, and exerting some independence (Mazel, 2020b). When new parents and those working in child-centered professions read "most children," they are implicitly evoking the concept of the "norm." If most children are toilet trained by age 3 or are beginning to read by age 6, then the message is that if a child is not reaching these milestones, their development falls outside the normative range and can be considered nonnormative or abnormal.

Developmental psychology has played a significant role in furthering the notion that ability can be objectively approached and the discipline has instilled "authoritative presumptions" (Vintimilla, 2018, p. 27) around expectations of what is appropriate for children at particular stages of childhood. Reconceptualist scholarship offers a contrasting view and challenges the pathologization within childhood developmentalism (Farley, 2018). For instance, "[t]he reconceptualist movement of early childhood education takes its cue from the aforementioned ideas to challenge the overreliance of developmental psychology in early learning contexts" (p. 10).

In disability studies, linear notions of developmentalism present a tricky tension. On one hand, it is critically important that a child's normative or nonnormative development be tracked so that appropriate interventions can be initiated. After all, the rights to early identification and intervention are enshrined within the Convention on the Rights of Persons with Disabilities (United Nations, 2006). If educators were to ignore a child's departure from typical developmental trajectories, in many cases, that would be considered a dereliction of duty. Interventions geared toward the Early Years can be of tremendous value to children and their families. However, the flip side, articulated by some in disability studies and disability activism, is that, at some point, the ongoing pressure to hone a particular skill set and continuous, rehabilitative interventions into a person's life can begin to negatively impact their sense of self-worth and quality of life.

Approaches to development that are understood as linear and espoused by developmental psychology are quite popular in traditional schooling. For children who do not meet identified developmental expectations, schools typically respond with stigmatized interventions that can powerfully shape the academic, social, and behavioral expectations of educators (such as many of those offered through special education). Education's adherence to the principles of linear development falsely assumes a universality in childhood experience. It also simultaneously narrows accepted pedagogical approaches to schooling. Linear and individual notions of developmentalism have been so deeply ingrained in our collective approach to education that its consequences often go unseen or are normalized. But it does not go unexperienced.

In many cases, highly sought-after behavioral, mobility, and psychological interventions have been reconceptualized as harmful toward the body, mind, and psyche of disabled people (Giangreco, 1996; Parens, 2006; Starr, 1982). For many children and their families, there is relentless pressure to pursue normalization through surgeries, therapies, and interventions. But when is "enough, enough?" When do we stop requiring people to conform to a constructed norm? When do we stop pushing for people to walk or talk in normative ways and instead acknowledge and embrace difference? This tension may be one of the most challenging to resolve within disability studies. However, it still remains an important tension for educators to hold in their work with students and their families.

How Educators Can Adopt More Holistic Developmentalism in Their Work

In education, there is an expectation that educators should have a working understanding of developmentalism, one that will inform educators' approach to classroom strategies, assessment, and behavior management. But educators can resist employing a deficit or pathology-oriented understanding of developmentalism by adopting frameworks that emphasize the relational context between children's development and the conditions in which they live and grow. When acting on assumptions related to developmental expectations, educators can draw from an array of theories that focus on social-relational and sociocultural approaches such as those forwarded by Vgotsky (Mahn, 1999) and Bronfenbrenner (Bronfenbrenner 1986/1992). There are also Indigenous understandings of childhood development that have a deep appreciation for cultural and historical contexts (ShadowWalker, n.d.). For example, the Public Health Agency of Canada released their report on Indigenous child, youth, and family health and described the rich context in which children's health and development should be considered.

> *Young Indigenous children experience many health disparities, which can largely be attributed to the socio-economic, environmental, political and historical conditions in which they live. High quality, holistic and culturally relevant ECD and care programs provide a promising avenue for addressing these health disparities by optimizing Indigenous children's physical, emotional, psychological, cognitive and spiritual development, giving them the best start in life and ultimately addressing health disparities over the long-term.* (Halseth & Greenwood, 2019, p. 7)

Family-centered models of child development and support are a popular approach in the Early Years (Mas et al., 2019). In the United States, the role of families is recognized as integral to early intervention strategies and enshrined in federal law (see IDEA and the development of Individualized Family Service Plan, United States Department of Education, 2017). Despite the holistic frameworks integrated into Early Years services and programs, there does seem to be a shift toward more-linear concepts of developmentalism within public education. This could be in part due to the organization of curricular expectations tied to the linear order of grades, and expectation of a linear trajectory as students move through school. But within those structural constraints, educators are still required to enact their own understanding of development and ability to measure students' achievement and report on their learning.

Ability-Grouping and Its Oppressive Effect on Students

While we all have a sense of what ability is, it's a complicated notion, particularly when applied to other people's children (Brantlinger, 2006). On a microlevel, ability is central to the many decisions educators make related to their practice. For example, when we enter a classroom, we might observe children studiously working in small groups, engaging with a particular text, or working together through a series of questions. The teacher might be circulating through the room, opting to sit down with one group or another as students take turns asking the teacher for points of clarification. This scenario may be a daily occurrence and appear to be routine. However, what remains unseen is how ability is the primary organizer of this activity. Those small groups of students scattered around the classroom may be intentionally organized by ability. If so, the texts they have been assigned to read or the concepts they have been asked to discuss are likely determined based on students' perceived level of ability. Student ability might also inform the time the teacher spends supporting and engaging with each group and which students they may select to work with one-on-one.

Ability-grouping can occur within the classroom, across programs (e.g. special education programs, gifted and talented programs, specialty and language immersion programs), across academic streams and tracks, and even across schools. In 2010, Dr. David Mitchell released an international review of empirical studies that looked at the benefits and pitfalls of both inclusive and special education practices. He released a second iteration of this review in 2015 and has published several books over his career. Studies included in Mitchell's reviews conclude that the act of ability-grouping students can result in serious negative consequences to students' learning—and not all of the consequences seem intuitive. For one, ability-grouping can significantly shape educators' expectations of students' ability. For instance, if a substitute teacher is told that their assignment will be carried out in the "MID intensive support class" (a self-contained class for students identified with mild intellectual disabilities), the name of the program, the association to a legacy of intelligence testing, the fact that these particular students have been extracted from the general education program and placed in an "intensive support" program, will very likely shape the educator's perception and expectation of students' ability. Conversely, if their assignment for the day was to take place in the "gifted" program, their expectation of how quickly they might work through the day's plans and the extent to which they might incorporate complexities and abstractness into their discussions could be influenced using similar inferences and clues based on labeling and historical concepts of intelligence.

Another critique of ability-grouping is that despite there often being a reduced number of students in "lower ability classes" and more one-on-one time with the teacher, studies show that generally, less work is completed and less curriculum taught in lower ability classes compared to mixed-ability classes (Houtveen & Van de Grift, 2001 as cited in Mitchell, 2015). Although the resources may appear to be in place to enhance student learning in special education classrooms, something about the formula of creating lower ability, standalone groups does not work to enhance student learning.

Based on earlier discussions around the conflation of race, class, and ability, a third critique is how students are organized along an ability hierarchy that very much mirrors our social, racial, cultural, linguistic, and class hierarchies (De Valenzuela et al., 2006; Mitchell, 2015). Also, from the discussion on the perception of "fixedness" of low ability as well as how ability is central to the organization of public education systems, it is likely not a surprise that many placements in low-ability classes are permanent (Houtveen & Van de Grift, 2001 as cited in Mitchell, 2015). This could be the result of a skills gap becoming increasingly stratified over time so that students may never reach a point in which they are deemed "able" or "caught up" enough to return to general education. It could also be that placement—on its own—formalizes perceptions and expectations of students' ability in such a fixed way that remaining in a low ability group seems neutral or natural.

Regardless of the evidence demonstrating its ineffectiveness in supporting lower achieving students, ability-grouping is still a hugely popular approach in public education. Ability-grouping allows schools to ignore structural factors associated with segregation and to place greater blame on students for academic failure. The rationale being that to be placed in a low-ability group, special education or elsewhere, students' learning must be compromised and, if compromised, their capacity for learning is likely perceived as unchangeable (Ladwig & McPherson, 2017). Therefore, regardless of pedagogy, if students are not reaching expected achievement milestones, it is easy to falsely assume that the "problem" lies only with them.

When we think about structural ableism, policies around ability-based organization are typically embedded at a system level, established by those in education who are largely removed from the day-to-day lived experiences of students. But when we organize students (and systems) based on assumptions of ability, students are rendered keenly aware of where they fit within the ability hierarchy of schools.

Once, when my eldest daughter was 9, I was working late into the night on a talk I was giving the next day on special and inclusive education. She was refusing to go to bed, so as many tired parents do, I made a deal. She could stay up so long as she listened to my talk and gave me some feedback. She happily grabbed a clipboard and pen and sat across from me while I went through what I was planning to say. The talk was about 15 minutes and as I was describing special education, her face fell. I wrapped up the rehearsal and asked what she thought. It seemed as though she was struggling for words; finally, she said, "I think we have something at our school just like what you described." She was visibly upset, so I asked her how she knew. She told me that, every once in a while, kids from another class would join hers, mostly for physical education. She did not know who they were, but she heard them called a "terrible" name—"special needs kids." I asked her what she thought that name meant, and she said she didn't know, but that it sounded like "something someone would call you if they were pretending to be your friend, but actually didn't like you."

She said that she didn't know why these kids were in special education, but that she saw that other kids weren't very nice to them. I asked her for an example. When they played soccer together out in the school field, she noticed that no one kicked them the ball. She confessed that no one kicked her the ball either, but she justified that that was because she was pretty bad at soccer. "These kids," she said, "looked like they would be really good at soccer and still no one kicked them the ball." This, to me, was a perfect illustration of how policy and practice shape the very real lived experiences of children, setting some up to participate and play, while setting others up for exclusion. Decisions on organization and labeling students through special education seemingly have nothing to do with physical education and social dynamics, but they do. The responsibility for ability-based organizational decisions fall entirely on the adults in the system, yet the consequences of these decisions are for children to bear. It is not the adult making the placement decision who is left standing on the sidelines of a soccer pitch, trying to play, and knowing no one will kick them the ball.

Policy decisions significantly contribute to classroom and school climate, and ability-grouping can lead to trauma. In fact, scholars have spoken out about ability-grouping as a form of symbolic violence (Archer et al., 2018). Likely, many of the students involved in ability-based practices, particularly low ability-grouping, have gone on to experience barriers in education, and yet, they are the ones that are asked to bear the implications of poor system planning and institutional failure. If anything, we have compounded the barriers students face by adding shame, humiliation, and discrimination to their day-to-day schooling activities. So when students enter into spaces where they encounter lower expectations and stigma, is it any wonder these spaces fail to produce academic success?

In our work with children and youth, it was clear that students are forced to grapple with the stigma produced by the distinctions constructed between able, unable, and disabled. In speaking to children about their experiences in a part-time special education program, many shared with us that their peers held highly negative views of the program. They reported that students thought special education was for kids who "knew nothing," were "r*tarded," "stupid," and "dumb." They spoke about kids being embarrassed by having to leave their class to go to a different room for extra help and how this led to them being treated differently by their friends and teachers. The pervasive theme across many of the interviews with children was just how bad they felt about being pulled out of class and treated differently from their peers based on the assumption that they were less capable. It hurt. And the stigma they experienced followed them from the classroom, to the playground, and all the way home.

Students spoke to how ability-grouping established a kind of hierarchy in schools. In high school, youth shared that Academic* courses were for "smarter" students so when they had to disclose to their peers that they were taking largely Applied-level courses, they felt judged and felt that others perceived them as "lower" and "different." Students reported that being at a different level of study created an awkwardness between themselves and their peers, a dynamic directly in response to how schools organize students. Another high schooler added that even though they were no longer in Applied, the fact that they had *ever been* had a lasting effect on how others perceived them. When they left Applied and moved into Academic-level courses, students reported feeling even more pressure to perform because others were expecting them to fail. They felt that they did not belong. Much like their younger peers in elementary special education, students who had experienced streaming agreed that the impacts of judgment and stigma were not limited to the boundaries of the school. Even friends and family would ask questions about why students were pursuing courses in the Applied level instead of Academic and encouraged them to switch

---

* In Ontario, courses in Grades 9–10 are typically offered at the Academic, Applied, and Locally Developed level, with Academic being the most academically comprehensive.

to an Academic level of study. From our interviews, these queries and encouragement to switch streams were often read as being judged.

When speaking to educators, they confirmed students' experiences of stigma as well. Many of them noted just how challenging it was on children to be singled out, particularly due to perceived low ability. Referring to students in special education, one educator noted that the students shared a sense of exclusion in the school and did not feel like they fit in at all. Another educator confirmed that students in special education are often viewed by their peers as being "less than" and that these persistent messages can ultimately be internalized. Educators reported that many students would act out because if they were going to be segregated from their peers, they would rather it be because, borrowing words from students, they were "bad" as opposed to "dumb." Educators attributed outbursts of behavior as a response to the pervasive sense of exclusion and to not being recognized, along with their peers, as a part of the class. Both students and educators spoke to us about the implications on students' self-concept and self-worth. Many interviews touched on the concept of *structural violence* where harm is unintended, but continues to be produced based on the structure of our systems. This cannot be the best option for children and youth. We must do better and reimagine systems that do not produce trauma and negatively effect students' schooling experiences.

Questions for Further Thought and Reflection

1. Educators are likely to encounter psychoeducational assessment reports as they review their students' files or IEPs. What steps can educators take to ensure that percentile information or statements like "low" or "slow" do not prevent them from holding high expectations for students?

2. In your school, what aspects of developmentalism are privileged? Is your school's approach to developmentalism multifaceted to ensure that children's physical, cultural, emotional, psychical, and intellectual development are considered? If not, how can you

broaden notions of development to embrace a more holistic view of child development?

3. Think through how your school addresses differences in abilities. What processes are implemented? What options for support are available? How are students typically organized and what role does ability play? What might this mean to students?

3

Detangling the Relationship Between Race, Class, and Perceived Ability

"Ableism is a systemic oppression that finds common ancestry with white supremacy."

—HAYDEN, 2020, PARA. I

There is a great deal of social justice work happening in classrooms and schools. In many instances, educators and administrators recognize the role schools and schooling practices play in advancing equity. It is also understood that schooling practices and approaches to teaching are not immune from biases related to race, class, gender, sexual orientation, and the like. However, less frequently discussed is how the perception of ability can be influenced by racism, classism, and other forms of discrimination. Ability is often attributed to certain configurations of bodies, cultures, classes—attributions frequently denied to others. When we think about why so many racialized children and/or children of minoritized cultures or of working-class parents are referred and placed in special education (Brown & Parekh, 2010; Connor, 2017; De Valenzuela et al., 2006; Ferri & Connor, 2005; O'Connor & Fernandez, 2006; Parekh & Brown, 2020; Skiba et al., 2006), we have to consider how special education and ability-based practices enable perceptions of students' ability to be influenced by racial, cultural, and class prejudice. We have to consider how how decisions to refer and place students in special education may be shaped by deep-seated biases and assumptions that certain children, from certain households, are somehow categorically different and less effective learners. Special education and, I would argue, all forms of ability-based programming, function as mechanisms through which racism and classism, in particular, can be enacted with little accountability (see Reid & Knight, 2006).

While the conflation between race, class, and ability often works to disadvantage minoritized groups, it can also work to benefit students who arrive to school with a significant degree of privilege. For example, students identified as gifted are more likely to be male, white, and wealthy (Parekh, Brown, & Robson, 2018). There are significant advantages to being perceived as having exceptionally high ability. Students identified as gifted are often afforded opportunities to learn in small, focused classes with high expectations, and they are believed to be deserving of perks and academic benefits. Students identified as gifted are more likely to experience a sense of belonging in school (Parekh, 2014) which could be derived, in part, from their knowing how valuable and valued their status of "gifted ability" is within education.

Whiteness and the Myth of Ability Neutrality

I grew up in a small urban area that was predominantly white. My home was a single dwelling, standalone house on a treelined street across from a local university. We were middle-class; my dad had a doctorate and held an established position in a prestigious medical school. My mom worked as a speech pathologist. Our neighbors were white and middle-class. In my small French immersion school, my classmates and teachers were mostly white. Our class trips were to largely white-run institutions, theaters, museums, and galleries. Our church congregation was predominantly white. Our family spent a lot of time in hospitals and doctors' offices where our physicians, interns, pharmacists, psychiatrists, psychologists, and nutritionists were white. We were effectively steeped in whiteness.

In fact, being inundated in whiteness lent itself to the presumption of neutrality. Our community's shared racial and class homogeneity made it seem as though any kind of observed "difference" was somehow objective. Homogeneity made difference feel explicit, distinctly defined, and tangible. You could almost point to it, draw an outline around it, and think "here, right here, is where the difference begins and where it ends." Perhaps racial and class homogeneity is what contributes to the fallacy that disability can be addressed as a singular issue, decontextualized from racialized or classed experiences. However, the experiences of disability within privileged identities and communities is still shaped through that privilege. Another reason why it is critically important to consider disability through an intersectional lens.

When it comes to schooling, ableism and racism are inextricably linked. For example, scholars argue that ability (or smartness) and whiteness are similarly constructed (Leonardo & Broderick, 2011). In schools and elsewhere, whiteness and smartness can be mobilized (or weaponized) to protect privilege. As discussed in Chapter 2, assessments used to determine smartness and ability have a history of "norm-testing" on white, middle-class children (Connor, 2017). Scholars argue that "[r]ace and disability have resided in the same social terrains throughout their history, especially so in educational territories. Eugenicist, modernist science has been instrumental in conflating the cultural topography of disability and race" (Smith, 2004, para. 52). As such, education has established ability-based processes that constructs ability through "whiteness as a normative, rationalist, modernist cultural structure (Smith, 2004, para. 32). Smith continues to explain that "[t]he normative disciplinary power of whiteness undergirding the rationality of Eurocentric culture and thought segregates not only those defined as not-white from the terrains of equality, equity, and justice, but also those defined as not-Able (body or mind)" (Smith, 2004, para. 98).

White spaces are not immune to racism just because discrimination is not being overtly expressed. In fact, white spaces and communities are often fastidious in their maintenance of and beholden-ness to whiteness. Creating intensively exclusionary spaces where ability-based norms and notions of neutrality are informed by whiteness. As such, white spaces can also be dangerous in their circulation of ableism and disability discrimination. Notions of normalcy are not only inscribed through whiteness; they are then used to disable and discount the presence, contributions, and value of racialized students.

Ableism hides in schools in the same ways that whiteness offers white communities a sense of neutrality. Many believe that schools offer the conditions for neutral assessment—but they do not. As Catastago (2014) writes, policies and practices enacted in schools are designed to protect whiteness. Similarly, in many schools, expectations for learning, behavior, and self-expression, including expressions of talent and engagement, have also been shaped by whiteness. Therefore, how could schools be neutral spaces?

Education tends to be much more comfortable with the idea that class can influence perceptions of ability, as a result of a lack of resources, than recognizing how perceptions of ability can be skewed by racial discrimination. If a student comes from a wealthy home where they have access to tutors, supports, and technology, they are more likely to perform better in school than a student who does not have access to the same material supports. But where it gets tricky is how quickly recognizing students' experiences of poverty can be reinterpreted with the suspicion of underlying impairment (Howard, Dresser, & Dunklee, 2009). Here again, the consequence for not meeting academic expectations, regardless of context, can result in the pathologization of students.

Positions of neutrality in education do not exist. We live and work in social and educational structures that uphold a legacy of colonialism and white supremacy. We are all shaped by our lived experiences, the environments within which we grew up, and the values that were embedded in the institutions of our youth. We have been immersed in messaging from schools, media, families, peers, work, and religious institutions; we have embodied positions on race, gender, ability, and class that cloud any attempts of neutrality. As educators, we must continuously reevaluate our assessments, our measures, and our perceptions of students' ability, checking and rechecking for how our ingrained biases are shaping our evaluation of others. Again, disability justice is only possible in solidarity with movements working toward racial, class, gender, and sexual justice.

Ableism and the Enactment of
Racism in Schools

Just as how our perceptions of ability can be influenced by bias, racism, classism, xenophobia, and other forms of discrimination, so can the assignment of ability-based categories and program placements. The theory of categorical inequality can be used to describe school-based practices and implications of categorizing students by perceived ability (Domina et al, 2017). "By creating categories and sorting youth among them, schools develop templates that influence the contours of inequality throughout contemporary societies" (Domina et al., 2017, p. 312). They suggest that creating educational categories, implicitly constructed around notions of ability, masks overt racism while, in effect, "co-construct[ing] racial categories" (p. 318) tied to ability.

Reid and Knight (2006) argue that the creation of school or special education–based categories plays an important role in justifying racial and class segregation while maintaining social inequality. They argue that racism and classism are enacted through practices of categorization and segregation on the basis of perceived normative/nonnormative ability.

> *"These so-called normal expectations justify teachers' holding students to standards that may not be familiar to those of non-European descent or even possible for students with impairments. Because most people in contemporary society perceive students with impairments as qualitatively distinct (i.e., empirically abnormal; Shapiro, 1999), "hunting for disability" in students—referral, diagnosis, labeling, sorting, and remediating—appears objective, fair, and benevolent (Baker, 2002). One result of perceiving "different" others through this technical–rational lens (i.e., as defective) is that it seems natural to many Americans that students of color, the poor, and immigrants lie outside the predominant norm and, therefore, belong in special education."* (Reid & Knight, 2006, p. 19)

Through the process of categorization, Reid and Knight (2006) argue that race, class, and immigration status become conflated with notions of ability and reinscribe racist, classist, and xenophobic assumptions of ability. This reinscription and conflation becomes so entrenched in our understanding of students, that no one seems surprised that their special education classrooms are disproportionately filled with Black, Indigenous, and Latinx students, as well as students from lower income homes. Using ability as a guiding characteristic also masks other forms of discrimination operating within schools. As Reid and Knight (2006) state, it is illegal to exclude students on the basis of racial identity or their family's income, but if it can be argued that their removal is based on ability, then the exclusion is somehow institutionally justified.

Examining Data on the Perception of Ability by Race, Gender, and Class

Before my current position as a research chair, I worked as a school district researcher. As system researchers, we examined district data for patterns of demographic disproportionality across programs and academic outcomes, including access to postsecondary education. From several of our studies, it was clear that racialized students, students living in poverty, and male students were overrepresented in special education and more likely to be bottom-streamed in high school. But data alone could not tell us how this was happening nor what took place when these placement or program decisions were being made. We had theories around why the outcomes were the way they were, but we struggled to "capture it" in a way that made sense. That was until we met a superintendent who was determined to uncover the same. This concerned superintendent wanted us to investigate how students were evaluated on their Learning Skills across students' identity characteristics. He claimed that this particular assessment had bothered him for some time and, he was sure, if we were to investigate it, there would be evidence of sweeping bias.

In Ontario, students from Grades 1–12 are evaluated on six identified Learning Skills: self-regulation, organization, responsibility, initiative, collaboration, and independent work (Ontario Ministry of Education, 2010). The evaluation of Learning Skills was designed explicitly to be subjective and untethered from student achievement. For instance, you could be a straight A student, but only receive a mark of "satisfactory" on "organization." Marks for Learning Skills were recorded as "Excellent," "Good," "Satisfactory," and "Needs Improvement."

The superintendent's concern was that *how* students' ability was perceived on these softer skills could ultimately shape approaches to pedagogy in the classroom. Based on their perceived ability, students might be guided toward different opportunities within school, offered different access to curriculum, and be directed towards different programs; all of which could shape students' success and trajectories through school. Convinced, we took it on.

We began with the premise that although reported Learning Skills marks did not *have* to correlate to students' achievement, we suspected there would be some relationship. After all, if students were demonstrating high achievement, they were also likely to be demonstrating "good" or "excellent" Learning Skills. And this was true. There was a strong relationship between achievement and how educators reported students' Learning Skills. Our second premise was that the relationship between achievement and Learning Skills should exist equally

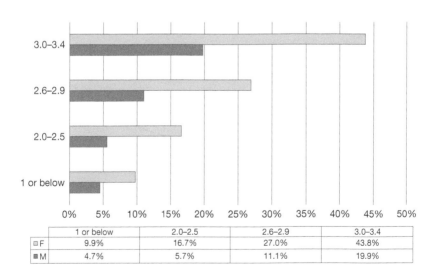

Figure 3.1 "Excellent" Evaluation on Learning Skills Across Gender and Achievement.

Source: Parekh, Brown & Zheng, 2018.

across all groups, and if it did not, results could be indicating potential evidence of bias.

We opted to use our provincial measure of achievement (see Education Quality and Accountability Office for more information) which reports student achievement in four levels. If a student is reported at a Level 1, it means they are really struggling with the material, Level 2 indicates a higher degree of proficiency at writing the test and engaging in the material. Level 3 has been identified as the provincial average. If students score a Level 3, they are perceived to be doing well. Students scoring Level 4 are the highest achievers. At the Grade 6 level, this assessment is conducted for mathematics, reading, and writing. Using these constructed levels of achievement, we selected students' Grade 6 provincial mathematics scores and examined their reported Learning Skill marks, breaking down by gender, racial identity, parental education acquisition, and special education programming. We chose to illustrate our trend data using only students who received a mean grade of "excellent" in their evaluation of Learning Skills and the results were stark (figures extracted from Parekh, Brown, & Zheng, 2018).

As you will notice in Figure 3.1, students who had scored 3.0–3.4 on their provincial Grade 6 mathematics assessment were the most likely to also be perceived as "excellent" learners, but despite having the same

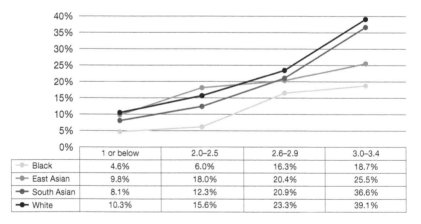

	1 or below	2.0–2.5	2.6–2.9	3.0–3.4
Black	4.6%	6.0%	16.3%	18.7%
East Asian	9.8%	18.0%	20.4%	25.5%
South Asian	8.1%	12.3%	20.9%	36.6%
White	10.3%	15.6%	23.3%	39.1%

Figure 3.2 "Excellent" Evaluation on Learning Skills Across Race and Achievement.

Source: Parekh, Brown & Zheng, 2018.

achievement, female students were over twice as likely to be reported as scoring "excellent" in their Learning Skills compared to their male peers. Note that at the time of analysis only male and female gender identities were available.

Disparities were also evidenced across students' racial identity. Again, looking at the category of the highest achievers included in Figure 2.3 (3.0–3.4), it is clear that white students were more likely to perceived as "excellent" learners on their Learning Skills compared to their South Asian, East Asian, and Black peers. In fact, white students were over twice as likely as Black students to receive a score of "excellent" despite demonstrating the same level of achievement.

Similar patterns also existed for students involved in special education (Figure 3.3). For reference, HSP (or Home School Program) represents students involved in a part-time special education program offered within their home school (orange bar), the blue bar represents students included in general education who have been formally identified through special education as having an exceptionality (excluding gifted) , and the green bar represents students who have never been involved in special education. Again looking at students who achieved at or above the provincial average (Level 3.0–3.4), students who were involved in a part-time special education program were least likely to be perceived as having "excellent" Learning Skills, followed by students who had been identified through special education. Students who had

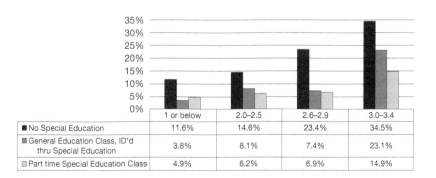

	1 or below	2.0–2.5	2.6–2.9	3.0–3.4
■ No Special Education	11.6%	14.6%	23.4%	34.5%
■ General Education Class, ID'd thru Special Education	3.8%	8.1%	7.4%	23.1%
▢ Part time Special Education Class	4.9%	6.2%	6.9%	14.9%

Figure 3.3 "Excellent" Evaluation on Learning Skills Across Special Education and Achievement. Source: Parekh, Brown & Zheng, 2018.

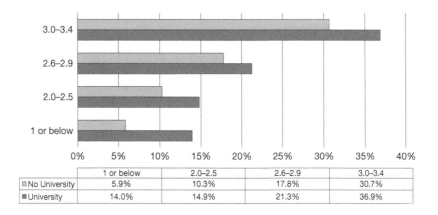

	1 or below	2.0–2.5	2.6–2.9	3.0–3.4
☐ No University	5.9%	10.3%	17.8%	30.7%
▪ University	14.0%	14.9%	21.3%	36.9%

Figure 3.4 "Excellent" Evaluation on Learning Skills Across Parental Education and Achievement. Source: Parekh, Brown & Zheng, 2018.

never been involved in special education were far more likely to score "excellent" on their Learning Skills despite *all three groups* reaching the same levels of achievement.

Lastly, we looked at students' parents' level of education, a factor often used as a proxy for class, and again, disparities existed despite students sharing similar achievement. Students whose parents had attended university were more likely to score "excellent" on their Learning Skills compared to their peers whose parents had not had the same postsecondary opportunities.

So in the end, female and white students, students who had never been a part of special education, and students whose parents had attended university were likely to be perceived as being excellent learners compared to their peers who identified as male, racialized students, students who had a history of special education, or whose parents had not attended university (see Parekh, Brown, & Zheng, 2018 for full results). Interestingly, the students that were privileged through these perceptual evaluations were female, white, nondisabled, and university-educated. Results urge us to think about who is primarily responsible for assessing students, particularly in elementary, and the role positionality might play in the perception of students' ability.

The results from the Learning Skills study are discouraging. They show that regardless of how hard students may be working in the classroom or at home, their *perceived* ability for learning is undermined by bias and discrimination. And it matters. These marks are not just used to complete a students' report card, they are often used to guide students toward a variety of academic opportunities. At one time, some schools opted to use students' Learning Skills (rather than reported achievement) to determine admissions to specialty programs, citing that it would be more fair and equitable to learners than using traditional curricular grades. Learning Skills are also used to support placement in special education or in lower academic pathways in high school. In other words, students' assessed Learning Skills have real-life consequences.

In fact, one of the most concerning factors is the relationship between educators' perception of students' ability and students' academic outcomes. The perceptions educators have of students' Learning Skills, reported as early as Grade 1, are incredibly strong predictors of students' access to postsecondary education over a decade later (Figure 3.5, presentation to the Ontario Public Supervisory Officers' Association, April 2021).

As the graph shows, the perception of students' Learning Skills in

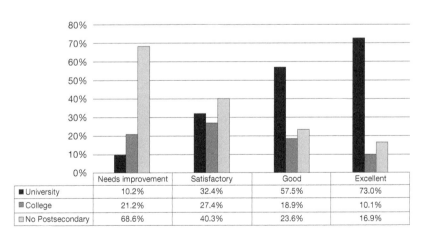

Figure 3.5 Grade 1 Learning Skills and Postsecondary Confirmations. Source: Presentation to the Ontario Public Supervisory Officers' Association, April 2021.

Grade 1 has a strong relationship with whether they will later access postsecondary education. Despite all the hailing of education being the "great equalizer," it is discouraging to think that children's academic trajectories can be set at age 6.

Listening to Students, Educators, and Administrators

Between roughly 2017–2019, our small research team conducted interviews across nine schools, each with highly diverse student populations. In our district, white students made up the largest racial group, but only accounted for around 30% of the overall student population within the system. Some schools we visited were in predominantly Black and/ or South Asian communities, other schools had student populations that were skewed more toward white and East Asian communities. But what remained consistent was that in asking to speak to students who had experienced lower level streaming or had been involved in special education, the majority of the students who signed up to participate in interviews were disproportionately Black and/or racialized. Students were keen to share that they, too, were well aware that racialized students made up a disproportionately large part of the lower streamed classes as well as of students placed on individual education plans.

Sitting around tables in various school conference rooms, students discussed how the role of race influenced the perception of ability. They shared that, in their schools, there was an overrepresentation of Black students in lower-level programming and in special education. Students also shared that they observed how white and East Asian students were more likely to access the best opportunities and receive the highest academic expectations and adulations. They suggested that the school worked well for white students, but not for them. In their observation, the school only privileged students who arrived with privilege. Whereas Black students, particularly Black students who lived in lower income communities, were "set up" to fail.

Students also shared where they believed things went wrong in the system, particularly contributing to why the performance of Black students continued to be undervalued and underappreciated in school.

The first issue they raised was how critical it was to have educators with lived experience of the communities they teach. Coupled with differences in racial demographics, students suggested that educators need to understand how access to resources differs across communities and that educators should not arrive with preconceived notions about access and performance. Students shared how assumptions around ability are then unfairly applied to students within the school, ultimately judging how students should be as opposed to meeting students where they are.

Students also acknowledged how educators unfamiliar with or without lived experience of the school or community often tend to resort to stereotypical engagement with curriculum or only cursory attention to the material that students, themselves, might find meaningful. For example, students shared how, in their experience, white educators may attempt to enter into discussions around Black history, but then often resort to discussions on slavery as though slavery were the only notable aspect of Black history. Students spoke at length about how exhausting discussions of slavery were and how much richer such discussions around Black history could be if led by those with community experience.

Biased assumptions around capacity not only result in the disenfranchisement of communities but they can also produce trauma for students and their families. Through our research, we spoke to a number of school administrators who shared that they observed that Black students and their families bore the brunt of pervasive ableist discrimination and the burden of low expectations and pathologization. Administrators spoke to how, in education, students are often pathologized when they do not behave or perform according to preconceived expectations of behavior or performance, and when expectations are not met, disability is the default assumption. And it does not stop with students. Families, too, are pathologized. Administrators also shared how current educational practices harken back to historical notions of eugenics and that the ongoing pathologization and exclusion of racialized and low-income students is essentially a eugenics-inspired repackaging of racist practices. In challenging racist and classist understandings of ability, we need to also look at what, and in what conditions, students are being asked to learn. Whose knowledges are represented in the classroom, within learning materials, and in curricular resources? Can students see themselves in their teachers and administrators in the school?

Culturally Relevant and Responsive Pedagogy

Ableism and racism have colluded together for generations to maintain inequality. The values of meritocracy, and whose "merit" counts, continue to be deeply embedded in public education. Culturally relevant and responsive pedagogy (CRRP) is supported by research as a key strategy to promote student achievement (MCauley, 2018). CRRP offers educators an opportunity to resist the pervasive influence of whiteness and/and as normalcy. Ladson-Billings (1995) describes culturally relevant pedagogy as drawing on similar tenets as critical pedagogy, particularly in that it is, as Freire discusses (2000), a "pedagogy of opposition" (p. 160). At its core, culturally relevant pedagogy includes three key experiences and aims: academic success, the development of cultural competence, and critical consciousness. Gay (2015) discusses the importance of teaching responsively and integrating students' histories, experiences, and cultural knowledges into the classroom. To teach responsively, educators can use the experiences and identities that students bring to school to help guide their decisions as to what material to integrate, which teaching strategies to adopt, how to approach the curriculum in a way that reflects and values the identities of students in their classrooms.

In discussions of culturally relevant and responsive pedagogy, students' identities play a central role. Typically, literature related to CRRP does not address nor include disability culture. The concept of disability culture has grown alongside the disability rights and justice movements and, for many, includes core tenets reflecting its cross-cultural nature. Members ascribing to disability culture may share similar histories of oppression, but also share a commitment to reorientating ideas about disability from deficit understandings to ones of empowerment (Dupré, 2012). Disability culture includes art, humor, positive representation, and focuses on a shared community (Dupré, 2012).

In interviews with secondary students, particularly in predominantly racialized communities, many shared that what was being taught in their classes had little relevance to their lives. There was a significant disconnect between what students valued and the material they were being asked to engage with in the classroom. Students spoke to the resulting boredom and disengagement and queried why material couldn't be more relevant to their lived experience. When selecting the types of material that will be posted to classroom walls—the book lists for the course's novel study, the examples used to help students deepen their learning—it is important to continuously ask: who benefits; who is excluded; and how might this relate and respond to the knowledges, experiences, and histories of students in the classroom?

Representation of community within the teaching staff is also important. Hiring educators that share students' knowledges, histories, and community experiences is key to promoting greater equity. It is important to employ educators who can deepen students' critical nature and who will enhance students' reflections and understandings of the multitude of oppressions they may face, as well as help them work through strategies for resistance. Effective educators can also take on an allyship role by working with students to dismantle barriers in public education, modeling a vision of equity within the classrooms they construct and the values they privilege.

Questions for Further Thought and Reflection

1. In your school, how are notions of ability racialized, classed, or gendered?
2. Which students are in your school's special education programs or are referred to special education? How are student demographics represented across academic streams? What are ways educators can disrupt patterns of racial and class disproportionality within special education or lower academic streams?
3. Does your teaching staff mirror the demographics of the school and community?
4. In what ways does your school practice culturally relevant and responsive pedagogy?

Part II

How Students Are Organized by Ability

4

Special Education Program, Identification, and Placement

"Individuals and groups who fail to achieve dominant standards are identified (marked, labeled, branded) with stigmatizing names (e.g. failure. . .at-risk) and sent to separated locations (special education rooms, low tracks, vocational schools). These distinction-making processes create a binary of (dominant) insiders and (subordinate) outsiders."

—BRANTLINGER, 2006, P. 200

U p to this point, we have largely explored how perceptions of ability are constructed. Chapters 4 and 5 will examine how these perceptions are formally institutionalized through special education and streaming systems. But one of the marked differences between special education and many other forms of ability-grouping is that its processes are largely enshrined in legislation. For instance, under federal US law, IDEA (Individuals with Disabilities Education Act) includes special education and states that children with disabilities can access free appropriate education (IDEA Section 300.101), least restrictive learning environments (IDEA Section 300.114), and early intervention (IDEA Part 303). In the United States, IDEA includes the provision of services and supports for infants and toddlers through the development of Integrated Family Service Plans (IDEA Section 303.344). In Canada, education is provincially mandated. In the province of Ontario, where my research is located, the Education Act covers K–12 schooling, although there are other provincial policies overseeing the Early Years.

Special education is historically steeped in medicalized notions of ability, exemplified by special education identifications (formal/ informal), prescriptive plans for remedy (IEPs), and treatment offered through supports in general education or placement in special education programming (Valle & Connor, 2010).

When I first began my career as a researcher, I was tasked to write a literature review that examined special education and the potential barriers special education practices presented for inclusion. The two most prominent themes to emerge from the literature were how special education identification processes and self-contained special education programming presented clear barriers to equitable practice and the promotion of inclusive academic opportunities.

Note that special education practices across the United States and Canada will differ in regulation, legislation, and law regarding practice and policy, but they are governed under similar objectives, principles, and approaches to ability and disability. Despite how controlled and legislation-heavy special education practices tend to be, special education processes are often fraught with complications and assumptions around expertise, professionalism, impact, and the assessment of ability. For instance, the implications of special education identification and programming are rarely discussed with families. Although there is a shared goal to support students in school and to help students "catch up," the reality is that students seldom catch up through special education intervention alone and that placement in special education programming often sets students along a permanent, downward academic trajectory (Parekh & Brown, 2019).

As a response to the antiquated practices in support and identification, Response-to-Intervention (RTI) was developed as a strategy systems can use to support students in the classroom and identify the degree of intervention that would be of most benefit (Martin, n.d.). The aim of RTI is to move forward with timely early intervention and evidence-based support, while reducing the number of students referred to the special education system. However, scholars argue that a successful RTI model must "ensure all students get what they need" (Ferri, 2016, p. 162) and break itself from the entrenched practices of diagnosing and removing students (Ferri, 2016).

Individual Education Plan/Program

Before getting into systems of identification and placement, let's first quickly review the individual education plan (IEP). (Note that IEP can also stand for individual education program as in the United States). In both the United States and Ontario, students in special education are entitled to an IEP. There are key differences between the IEP in the United States and IEPs in Ontario. In the United States, IEPs are legally binding, meaning that the services, accommodations, and modifications included within the IEP must be met by the school or system. In Ontario, IEPs are required to be created for every student formally identified through an Identification, Placement and Review Committee. Although services, accommodations, and modifications are included in students' IEPs, schools and districts are not bound in the same way that they are in the United States. Another key difference is who creates the IEP. In the United States, the IEP is created by an IEP team that includes the child's parent, a minimum of one of the child's general education teachers and a minimum of one of the child's special education teachers, someone who can interpret assessment results, a representative from the district as well as the child (once they are 16 years of age). Other individuals and representatives can also be invited to attend (IDEA Section 1414 D; Center for Parent Information and Resources, 2017; Understood Team, n.d.). Attendance of IEP team members may not be required should it be agreed that the member's area of expertise, curriculum or service is not up for discussion or modification (IDEA Section 1414 D). In Ontario, IEPs are typically created and/ or updated by the child's teacher or special education teacher, ideally in partnership with the child's guardian or parent, and in consultation with any specialized services offered through the district. However, the school's principal has ultimate responsibility for the IEP (Ontario Ministry of Education, 2004). As with all education policy, its enactment can sometimes differ across systems and schools.

Across both the United States and Ontario, IEPs include important information around what types of services or accommodations a student may be entitled to, what modified curricular expectations students are working toward, as well as listing the types of assessments and evaluations the student has undergone and considerations for transition planning (IDEA Section 1414 D). The IEP is intended to function as a central planning document and should be incorporated into the pedagogical planning in the classroom. However, due to the nonbinding nature of IEP recommendations in Ontario, parents frequently raise concerns around the IEP being ignored, forgotten from year-to-year, and only implemented when a problem arises or at the discretion of the educator. In theory, the IEP is intended to ensure educators have a clear understanding of what students need to be successful in the classroom and how they are obligated (US) or recommended (Ontario) to support. But IEPs have the reputation of being an "add-on" to classroom program development and a source of extra, inequitably distributed work for educators. They have also become a flag for disability or inability and have been consequently stigmatized.

When we spoke with students in Ontario about special education and the function of an IEP, students spoke directly to the stigma they experienced by having an IEP as part of their learning plan. When asked about the types of guidance they received in selecting courses for high school, students shared that having an IEP and/or attending resource meant you were excluded from selecting Academic level courses for high school, leaving many students ineligible to pursue university education in the future. Other students also shared that they had experienced direct exclusion in the classroom in relation to their IEP. They reported that, due to their IEP, they were frequently asked to leave the classroom during more interesting activities to attend resource.

Students also saw IEPs as a form of punishment and judgment on not just their academic achievement, but on their social relationships in school, and as a tool for social control. Students reported that if you got involved with the "wrong crowd," for example, students who were already on IEPs, your proximity to this group could also result in being presumed that you, too, required an IEP. IEPs can serve as important documents that track and monitor students' progress through programs and record key information around accommodations and modifications. However, it is critical that we understand that they can also carry and perpetuate tremendous stigma—stigma that children are left to navigate on their own.

Special Education Identification

In the United States, there are 13 disability categories covered under IDEA. These areas include specific learning disability, other health impairment, autism spectrum disorder, emotional disturbance, speech or language impairment, visual impairment (including blindness), deafness, hearing impairment, deaf-blindness, orthopedic impairment, intellectual disability, traumatic brain injury, and multiple disabilities (United States Department of Education, 2017). For students whose disability-related needs are not recognized elsewhere, there is a broader civil rights law, Section 504 of the Rehabilitation Act (1973), that can be invoked to address disability discrimination in school and ensure students are supported in school (United States Department of Education, 2020).

In Ontario, there are 12 similarly recognized exceptionalities that fall under umbrella categories of behavior, communication, intellectual, physical, and multiple exceptionalities. A quick reminder, Ontario uses the term *exceptionalities* within its special education system as opposed to *impairment* or *disabilities*, in part, because its system also includes the identification and support of children identified as gifted. For Ontario-based students whose needs are not being recognized or met by district special education processes, there is also the Ontario Human Rights Code, which prevails over provincial legislation to ensure that all students with disabilities are accommodated in school (Ontario Human Rights Commission, 2008/2018). However, the process involved in pursuing a human rights case related to disability discrimination and accommodations can be lengthy and complicated.

For each system, there is a process through which students undergo evaluation or formal assessment to determine eligibility for special education supports. In the United States, the process includes initial evaluations, reevaluations, and independent education evaluations (IEEs) (Washington Office of Superintendent of Public Instruction, n.d.). Once students are determined to be eligible for special education services, an IEP is created and placement is established. Similarly, in Ontario, the process for evaluation and placement is overseen by an Identification, Placement and Review Committee (IPRC). However,

Ontario's education system is able to provide IEPs for students without a formal identification of exceptionality or disability and without having to go through the more formal IPRC process.

Although educational systems have processes of evaluation and identification to identify which students are eligible to receive resources and services, tying access to a system of identification can be challenging. Evaluation groups often include or are led by professionals with expertise in education, special education, or psychology, but, in the end, they may have little direct knowledge of, or relationship with, the student.

Complicating Institutional Identification and Self-Identification of Disability

When we think about disability as identity, an identity someone may ascribe to for life, the process of institutional identification carries significant weight. But when it comes to the evaluation and identification of ability, special education committees are not neutral. As discussed in Chapter 3, assumptions around students' ability and capacity can be shaped by other forms of bias and discrimination. Aside from the extent that bias can shape the outcome decisions of evaluation boards or committees, the categories of disability or exceptionality are, themselves, problematic. For one, serious concerns have been raised around the origin, continued relevancy, and archaic nature of currently used definitions of disability categories (Reid et al., 2020). There is a flawed sense of homogeneity among categories of identification (Mitchell, 2015) that does not exist in the lived experience of disability. Identification categories also offer educators limited information in terms of actual pedagogy or how to support students in the classroom. For instance, if, as an educator, I am told that a child in my class has been identified as having a learning disability, the label alone does not provide me with enough information to know how best to accommodate or differentiate my instruction. Students identified within disability or exceptionality categories are diverse and will require an array of strategies to support. The only way to know what a student needs in the classroom is to know the student—a label is insufficient.

The disability rights and justice movements continue to gain momentum. As such disability is more often being recognized as an identity, challenging notions that disability is only understood as impairment. Therefore, the power of evaluation or identification groups to identify and ascribe identity characteristics to children may be largely out of sync with children's lived experiences of disability.

As noted in Chapter 1, a colleague and I just completed a recent study that explored a large population of students, all identified through special education. We looked to uncover whether these same students *also* identified as someone with a disability (Parekh & Brown, 2020). The disconnect was astounding. Overall, less than a third of students identified through special education, actually self-identified as having a disability. This varied across category of disability or exceptionality, racial identity, gender, and other identity characteristics (for more see Parekh & Brown, 2020). Additionally, many students who self-identified as disabled were not formally identified through special education.

These results show that there is a critical chasm between how youth understand disability and the understanding of disability in education. Reframing disability as an identity has significant implications on the work of evaluation or identification groups. Assigning an identity label to another human, a label they will likely carry for a lifetime, to which they may neither agree nor ascribe to, should raise critical ethical questions and concerns for all of us involved in education.

Implications of Institutional Identification Processes

The implications of an institutional identification are real and often have significant material consequences (Fonseca & Zheng, 2011; Irwin, 2015; Kearney et al., 2015). In my work, it has been evidenced that students who are identified as having a Mild Intellectual Disability (MID) are likely to be removed from the general program, streamed into lower academic programs in high school, and rarely make it on to postsecondary (Parekh, 2014). Unlike a physical impairment, the identification of an MID can be determined through psychoeducational assessments, but as we learned through our interviews, can also be based on the impressions educators and administrators have around students' ability. Categories like MID are considered "judgmental" categories (Artiles et al., 2010, p. 281) as they are highly susceptible to bias. Persistent racism may explain why, in our study, proportionally, Black children are two and a half times more likely to be identified as having an MID (Brown et al., 2021).

One of the recurrent themes that emerged from our work with educators around special education identification is a sense that there is a degree of arbitrariness to the labels. From our interviews, we heard accounts of MID identifications, particularly those ascribed to Black children, that were determined by IPRC committees, despite the absence of supporting or conclusive documentation. As such, administrators raised serious questions as to who ends up referred, labeled, and moved through the special education system and who is understood as a low performer in school. When we spoke to administrators, they shared how a special education identification significantly influenced how educators perceived students' ability, regardless of achievement. They observed that when a child arrived to class with a label attached, the immediate perception was that they would have a low ability to perform or achieve. Yet in many classes, there would be several students who also demonstrated similar low achievement or performance, but their ability was not constructed nor pathologized like their peers who were identified through special education.

Of course, all educators expect to have students in their classroom, who, for a variety of reasons do not perform at grade level. Even though educators have a series of tools in their toolbox to reach low-performing students, when low performance is coupled with a special education label, educators may believe that they do not have the right tools to reach that student. In many cases, the label has rendered that child categorically different. So what makes the difference? How do some students move through the system with low achievement being left just as they are, while the low achievement of others is pathologized and addressed through removal and placement in special education? For many white, middle-class/upper-class families, special education can offer opportunities to establish key accommodations and supports. As Reid and Knight (2006) identified, of disabled students accessing post-secondary education, the majority are from white families who earn over a six-figure salary. When we look more closely at how students are identified, wealthier, white students are much more likely to be identified as having a learning disability or autism, whereas racialized students are disproportionately overrepresented in the category of MID. Being identified as having a learning disability or high-functioning autism not only presumes intellectual capacity or even brilliance, but also is deeply medically rooted as depicted by the many neuroscientific studies that map neuroactivity, dyslexia, for example, and reading. Compared to MID, where the connotation is overall low ability often coupled with suspicions of possible impairment as a result of poor parenting, neglect, or poverty. These are highly racialized and racist frames of ability and further indicate the inextricability of white supremacy and ableism. The way populations are stratified across impairment identification also speaks to what Waltz & Schippers (2020) describe as the *hierarchy of impairments*; a term

> *used to describe how perceptions of and attitudes toward disabled people often depend on the type of impairment they have and how it occurred (Hernandez, Keys, & Balcazar 2000; Deal 2003). Whether an individual's impairment is viewed positively, negatively, or as a neutral factor depends largely on cultural factors, so this will vary between countries, but there is a rich literature indicating that persons with cognitive impairments are typically judged as less deserving than those with physical or sensory impairments. (for example, Thomas 2000; Harpur, Connolly, & Blanck 2017, p. 9)*

When such connotations of ability are attached to racial identity and racist notions of capacity, they co-construct categories of ability.

> *. . . disabled people (as well as nondisabled parents, teachers, and members of society in general) often perform hierarchies whereby they denigrate certain exceptionalities as having lower status, and in the process valorize others, such as the cultural preference for Asperger*

*over autism, or high-functioning over low-functioning autism (gen-
erally accepted popular cultural codes for "smart" and "not-so-smart"
autistics). Often, these strategies develop as learned defensive responses
against the larger and threatening presence of Whites in the case of
race, or the normate in the case of ability. That being said, they
unwittingly reproduce the system of stratification responsible for their
degradation.* (Leonardo & Broderick, 2011, p. 2222)

These competing and coreplicating hierarchical structures ensure that
students and their families are always on unequal ground in terms of
their social position within schools, as to whether or not they "belong,"
or how much power they are granted to challenge the school's response
to their child.

Ability-Grouping and Special Education Programming

Self-contained programming is one of the most hotly debated aspects
of special education. Despite the disability rights movement's push for
greater inclusion in school and the reduction of self-contained programming, it is important to note that special education, as a system,
has actually expanded and become more diffuse. Special education
identification used to be less common, but has been steadily growing.
In 1976–1977, American data shows that 8.3% of students were served
under IDEA, which grew to 13.7% for 2017–2018 (National Center
for Education Statistics, 2018). In our local district, the proportion of
students involved in special education now hovers between 18%–20%,
or approximately 1 in 5 students (Brown et al., 2013; 2021). In addition
to the expansion of the special education system, there has been a substantial expansion in the professionalization of special education and
the psychologization of learning. While special education may look
somewhat different now compared to when the civil rights and disability rights movements shone a spotlight on its role in disability discrimination and inequality, it is still a vast system currently operating
in public education.

Historically, self-contained programming served several purposes.
During the height of eugenics era, keeping disabled children separated
from their peers followed similar logics to larger social patterns at the

time. Key capitalist logics of efficiency were also used to justify the segregation of disabled students. As Danforth and colleagues (2006) wrote, "By clearing out the weak and disruptive students, schools could become more efficient in the delivery of curriculum to the nondisabled students" (p. 15). Under capitalist logic, disabled children are perceived to present as barriers to school efficiency, and special education seemed to offer a solution—remove and move on.

Addressing the history of segregation, Danforth, Taff, and Ferguson (2006) describe how "place" was once thought to be "both a social reform and an individual remedy" (p. 5) where there were therapeutic benefits to the sole act of bringing disabled people together in a separate space. They spoke of this justification as "curative geography" (p. 4) where place was, itself, considered to have therapeutic qualities. Although in the past, proponents of segregation argued that place supported the creation of a "therapeutic community" (p. 5), what resulted in schools was not a community developed through the self-determination of students. Instead, segregated spaces were emblematic of "an isolated, artificial and professionalized configuration" (p. 5). In the education of disabled children, place is often treated as a critical component of curriculum. The idea that certain disabled children should be taught together—outside of general education—continues to be a foundational tenet of special education.

Geography is an interesting way to conceptualize the values of a school. When I teach in the Faculty of Education, I often ask teacher candidates to share where different classes or programs are housed in either the schools they attended as students or in the buildings where they are conducting their practicum placements. Many students report finding special education programs housed in separate wings of a school or in the school basement—the trend is that these classes are housed away from others. This is not by accident.

For a very small proportion of students in special education, the aim of a special education program may include access to alternative curriculum, life skills, skills that prepare students to enter the labor market directly from school, and access to different therapies and services. In these cases, special education is imagined more as a day program for students as they transition into adulthood. For the vast majority of students in special education, special education is intended to be timed-limited support or programming, where students receive intensive remediation, and then return to general education. If this were so, then the idea of self-contained special education programs makes a lot of sense. That is, when you have a handful of children who are struggling with a particular skill or several skills, you bring them together with intensified resources, expert educators, and targeted intervention. With students rotating in temporarily and then back out to their general education class, a self-contained program should yield positive academic results.

Unfortunately, few of these aims are ever realized. As described in Chapter 2, research shows that, despite these self-contained, high-resource programs, students generally have *less* access to curriculum and that placement in special education offers few pathways back to the general education program (Mitchell 2010; 2015). Studies have also shown that students in inclusive settings are more likely to reach greater independence than are students in special education settings (Parekh, 2013). In our own qualitative work, it was clear that many students did not like being a part of special education. They shared that being associated with special education made them feel badly about themselves. Some even articulated that, once they realized they had been placed in a low-ability group, their subsequent academic failure had been a personal choice to live *down* to the school's low expectations of them.

From our work in special education, we also learned that unless administrators were purposively hiring skilled educators to work in special education, expert educators were more likely to be allocated to enriched programs, with special education being staffed by those willing to take the position. Self-contained special education programs are tremendously difficult to staff. Education leaders and special education staff have commented that teaching in special education carries a certain professional stigma. Within our large urban district, teachers were frequently and eagerly seeking jobs within the system. While there may be a few grade/subject jobs available each hiring cycle, there were frequently positions in self-contained special education programs that were difficult to fill. Additionally, special education programs are notoriously understaffed, and many staff experience the sense that, once they sign up, they are isolated and on their own.

There are also calls to address self-contained special education programs because of safety concerns (Westoll, 2017). Administrators were reporting that self-contained programs were becoming increasingly unruly. Even when special education programs were designed for students with learning disabilities, administrators shared that some self-contained classrooms were becoming more difficult to manage. Rarely did these conversations problematize what ability-based segregation feels like to a child or what it feels like to continuously face low expectations. For some children, negative behaviour, or at least what is interpreted as negative behaviour, is actually a form of resistance and communication.

Problematizing Ability Grouping Through District Data

There seems to be a continued misunderstanding of successful models of learning. Research is showing that children often learn more from their peers than from the educator at the front of the room (Mitchell, 2010). This learning can be supported by group work that provides intentional opportunities for students to discuss and collaborate together. But students who are in self-contained programs are at a disadvantage in accessing the same diversity of ideas and skills as students in a general program.

My own district data shows that students identified with a learning disability and enrolled in the general program fare far better academically than students with the same designation enrolled in a self-contained program (Brown & Parekh, 2010). When my colleagues and I later presented these findings, it was surprising to us how quickly they were dismissed, by some, as merely reflecting the lack of capacity of students in special education programs. We were told repeatedly that these disparities made sense. In their opinion, not only did our findings confirm that programs have been appropriately organized, by enrolling the most severely impaired students into self-contained programs, but that students' lack of success, in the end, had everything to do with students' lack of ability. In other words, they believed that the structure and aims of the program were successful; it was the students who were failing.

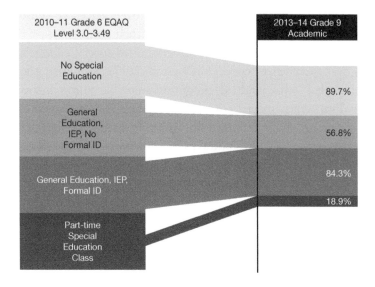

Figure 4.1 Relationship Between Achievement, Special Education Placement, and Access to Secondary Programming. Source: Parekh & Brown, 2019.

Troubled by this, my colleague and I conducted a study examining program outcomes related to how students were organized by perceived ability. For this study, we held achievement constant (as determined through provincial testing, adjudicated externally to the school) and then tracked, by program structure, the academic trajectories of students. We discovered that students whose achievement scored near or at the provincial average and were *not* involved in special education, had close to a 90% chance of enrolling in key academic secondary programs that would set them up for opportunities to pursue postsecondary education. For students who had the *same* level of achievement, but were enrolled in a part-time special education program, they had less than a 20% chance of enrolling in the same key secondary program of study (see Parekh & Brown, 2019 for more and additional figures).*

* Note that there are currently 72 school districts in Ontario. The data examining special education is taken from one Ontario school district that supports close to a quarter of a million students.

The outcomes of this study, debunk the myth that poor special education outcomes can be solely excused by low student ability and highlights the need to consider how the structure of special education may
be playing a significant role in student achievement.

When we explored the demographics of which students were being
placed in this particular part-time special education program, our
findings essentially confirmed what the larger international body of
research was showing (De Valenzuela, et al, 2006; Artiles, et al., 2010;
Connor, 2017). In our case, students placed in this part-time special
education program were more likely to not have a formal identification of disability, were disproportionately Black or from lower income
families, and were the most likely to have parents who, themselves, had
never had the opportunity to access postsecondary education. Since we
confirmed that ability only partly explained pathway outcomes, we felt
that the study's findings were further evidence of the social and cultural reproduction function of schools.

Educators we spoke to confirmed that parents were generally
told that by placing their child in a special education program, they
would receive specialized attention, instruction, and the tools needed
to close any academic gaps. These same educators also acknowledged
that what parents were seeking in terms of remediation and what they
believed their child was receiving through special education does not
exist. They noted that parents were typically told that special education will offer intense, remedial programming in a small-group setting
and that it will enable their child to "catch up" so they can return to
their general program. But that doesn't typically happen. Educators
observed that once these gaps were established, they were never successfully bridged through special education programming. From the
perspective of the educators, special education was not achieving the
ends intended—a conclusion supported by international research as
well (Mitchell, 2015).

Student, Educator, and Administrator Perspectives on Special Education

Perhaps, in part, the failure of self-contained programming may stem
from its impact on students. When we asked educators how students

feel about moving from self-contained special education programming to more inclusive classrooms, educators reported that, overall students preferred being part of the general class and did not enjoy being singled out to leave for special education programming. Educators shared that having students leave the general education program for special education support resulted in those students missing out on being a part of the classroom culture and significantly hindered their cohesion in the classroom. They reported that many schools are not set up to enable students to flourish academically and, as a result, students internalize failure and begin to believe that their inability to learn is their fault. This internalization of failure is further reinforced through low expectations and the assignment of "coloring pages" to students who could be challenged with more engaging work. Educators also shared that when given high expectations, students will rise to the challenge, and when they are valued within the class, they "shine."

For younger students, leaving their homeroom for part of the day resulted in losing out on opportunities to build community in the class, such as missing out on jokes, celebrations, and shared classroom experiences. When children are separated from their peers during the day for intensive programming, it is assumed that learning is directed from educator to student and that peer support plays a secondary role in students' engagement in material. As mentioned earlier, learning is a social and relational activity. Students reported to us that they learn better from their peers because their friends can explain instruction in a way they can more easily understand. When we polled our middle school student interviewees, ALL said they preferred an inclusive placement compared to attending a special education program.

From our research with educators and their experiences with students and their families, it was clear that parents and children held reservations around being pulled out of the general program and placed in a self-contained special education program. One of the schools involved in our research had recently reorganized their special education programs and reintegrated students in special education back into the general classroom. We had arrived at the school shortly thereafter, when the transition was fairly new. Curious as to how the integration was going, we asked educators how families were adjusting to what many perceived, at the time, as a loss of support. An educator shared with us that, overall, parents were really supportive and "happy" that their children were no longer being removed from the classroom to attend a special education program. From their perspective, parents wanted their children to be included in their homeroom class. It is unclear what parents understood about special education when they were advocating for inclusion, but it was evident that special education programming was somehow connected to isolation and exclusion.

We cannot ignore that, for many families, the process of special education is one of trauma and, at times, mired in mystery. The points where families can intervene in the special education process are generally governed by professionals, special education consultants, psychologists, educators, and administrators who all share a similar language and insider knowledge of the special education system. Outside the Early Years, the influence of families on special education decisions can be limited, and our interviewees believe that families have been intentionally excluded to facilitate the aims of the system.

Even when families are at the "right" tables to discuss their child's IEP, programming, and accommodations, do the special education teams share the community or cultural experiences of the families they are serving? What kind of language is being used in those meetings? Special education itself has developed an opacity through its development and implementation of specialized language that only "insiders" can understand. From interviewing administrators, "insider" language is pervasive in meetings with families. This can leave families unclear as to what is really going on and to the potential implications of the decisions being made. Our interviewees shared that even when families are present and well-versed in the system, instead of consulting or co-constructing special education guidance, they are often talked at or talked through, reducing their power to influence special education decisions. As interviewees pointed out, families are often sold an idea of special education that will never come to fruition, and they are kept in the dark about the lasting implications special education may have on their child's future. As one administrator claimed, families are sold the idea that special education is a fix, but it is not. And, if families knew the implications of special education, "nobody would come."

Questions for Further Thought and Reflection

1. In your school, how is special education presented to families? In terms of outcomes, what are families told?
2. Thinking through the identification and placement processes, what challenges do families encounter and what are ways that educators can support families?
3. What does it mean to be an advocate for families? What role can advocates play in supporting families through the special education system?

5

Academic Streaming and Hierarchies of Ability

"The legitimacy of setting is maintained through misrecognition, in which students come to understand themselves and others as 'deserving' their set allocation on the basis that the judgements used to assign them are simply reflective of their 'natural' abilities and that segregation is needed in order to protect (to legitimate and not contaminate) the ('better') experiences and attainment of those with higher 'ability' from the 'distracting' presence of 'others' (those of 'undesirable' ability, disposition and behaviour)"

—ARCHER, ET AL., 2018, P. 136

Academic streaming* (tracking, as it is referred to in the United States) is what occurs when students are guided toward specific ability-based program pathways, typically related to the academic level (courses or programs) students select upon entering high school. However, in many ways, these ability-based pathways can also begin as early as kindergarten (e.g. special education or specialized programming) and are, in part, responsible for the vastly different outcomes students experience following high school. There are significant jurisdictional differences in the United

---

* *Academic tracking* is generally a term used in the United States to describe the distinct pathways through which students are guided through education. The synonymous term in Canada is *academic streaming*. Intended to be subject specific, setting follows the same logics as tracking/streaming (see Archer, et al., 2018).

States and Canada in how streaming is organized in public education. But regardless of pathway names, how explicit or diffuse systems are, or how districts decide to organize their student population, there are shared underlying assumptions that continue to maintain elements of streaming across public education systems.

Jeannie Oakes is a prominent US scholar on education tracking. She describes tracking as follows:

> *Tracking is the process whereby students are divided into categories so that they can be assigned in groups to various kinds of classes. Sometimes students are classified as fast, average, or slow learners and placed into fast, average, or slow classes on the basis of their scores on achievement or ability tests. Often teachers' estimates of what students have already learned or their potential for learning more determine how students are identified and placed. Sometimes students are classified according to what seems most appropriate to their future lives. Sometimes, but rarely in any genuine sense, students themselves choose to be in "vocational," "general," or "academic" programs.* (Oakes, 2005, p. 3)

Essentially, students are organized by ability, real or perceived, along pathways that lead to disparate post-high school outcomes.

Prior to entering high school, students often select, or have selected for them, the academic pathway they will pursue in their secondary studies, often aligned with what they hope to pursue in the future. Pathways often result in vastly different postsecondary outcomes, with some students graduating high school with no or limited options to pursue further education. In Ontario, course levels in Grades 9–10 are called Academic,* Applied, and Locally Developed, shifting into University, Mixed, College, and Workplace streams for Grades 11–12. Embedded into the narrative of student choice is the idea that, should students select a pathway that is not a good "fit," they can always transition to a pathway that better aligns with their grades and approach to school. However, with prerequisite requirements and limited available

---

* Note that the highest academic stream in Ontario's Grades 9–10 general education programming is named "Academic." Thus, when referring to specific programming level "Academic" will be capitalized. When referring to academic or academics more broadly, "academic" will be in lowercase.

bridging courses, it can be challenging to transition into more rigorous programming compared to transitioning into lower academic courses. Therefore, once students begin their high school trajectories, we find that pathways are fairly complete (Parekh, 2014; Parekh et al., 2021). In terms of post high school destinations, it is important to note that "[b]oth the US and Canada have colleges and universities, but the terms have different meanings . . . In Canada, there is a big difference between the two: universities grant degrees, while colleges grant certificates and diplomas. In Canada, a college is similar to institutions called "community college" in the United States (Shorelight team, 2021, para 9–10).

Streaming is often discussed as an organizational strategy aimed toward supporting students and easing pedagogical challenges in the classroom. But at the root of academic streaming is ableism, shaping how we think about and respond to ability. As Oakes (2005) describes, the purpose of streaming is to parse the student population by ability and align their perceived ability to a prescribed ability-based course structure. As Oakes points out, how students are classified and, subsequently, their recommended placement, can be based on others' perceptions of what types of vocations they believe a student will be best suited for, their assessment of a student's prior learning or educational experiences, or of how they assess a student's potential for learning in the future (Oakes, 2005).

Streaming and its Relationship with Postsecondary Education

The academic program that students pursue in high school can either enable or disable their future access to postsecondary education. When I describe this consequence to groups or classes, the first response I generally hear is "what about students who want to pursue a vocation in the trades? They won't need Academic or University preparation courses to get there." While this may seem intuitive, we are uncovering that pathways marked for particular postsecondary destinations are not graduating students eligible to pursue their desired postsecondary programs.

Another troubling trend is that most new jobs, including jobs in the trades, will require some postsecondary (particularly college level) education. Pathways through high school that lead to jobs in the trades and toward apprenticeships should be equally as valued and supported as pathways leading to college or university. But most importantly, all pathways, including those for apprenticeships and trades, should ensure students reach their desired destinations.

Tracking the System

The structure of streaming is complex. Although organization across districts can differ, schools generally follow a particular pattern. Working backwards, postsecondary education institutions generally regard students' Grade 11 and 12 transcripts as part of their evaluation of eligibility for admission. In terms of structure, Grades 11 and 12 courses are generally more specialized toward postsecondary destinations than are Grade 9 and 10 courses, which are typically more generalist. But even though they may be more generalist in content, the level of courses taken in Grades 9 and 10 can determine what students are eligible to select particular Grades 11 and 12 courses.

For context, in 2011–2012, approximately 66% of all students entering Grade 9 entered into the Academic stream, with 25% in the Applied stream and 4% in the Locally Developed stream. Both Academic and Applied streams are intended to lead students toward postsecondary education (university and college) (Parekh, 2013). Yet, findings from a cohort study later revealed that the majority of students entering Academic in Grades 9–10 went onto Grade 11–12 University prep courses and then to university. In contrast, of students who entered the Applied stream in Grades 9–10, most students took Grade 11–12 College prep courses—a presumed postsecondary pathway. But, less than 40% of students taking College-level courses actually went to college—with roughly the same proportion not even applying to postsecondary education. The majority of students who accepted an offer to an Ontario college had actually taken the majority of their courses at the University-prep level (Quan & James, 2017; To, et al., 2017). These outcomes were measured after 6 years from when students entered high school in Grade 9. Examining records of all secondary students after 4 years of high school (essentially students who graduated "on time"), only 11% of students who started Grade 9 in the Applied track had confirmed an offer to an in-province college and 4.2% to a university. In contrast, after 4 years of high school, students who entered Grade 9 in the Academic stream had an acceptance rate of 55% for an in-province university, 5% for college (Parekh, 2013). For students entering Grade 9 taking the majority of their courses at the Locally Developed level, there is a very limited chance of accessing any form of postsecondary education following high school (Figure 5.1).

The proportion of students in the Locally Developed/Workplace stream has increasingly come to be students with a history of elementary special education. Even though special education programs exist in high school, students identified through special education constitute close to two thirds of students pursuing the Locally Developed/Workplace stream (Parekh, 2013). These statistics should raise concerns about structural discrimination in which disabled students are knowingly guided toward programs that offer little to no opportunity for future education.

As Oakes (2005) noted, what drives pathway decisions has a lot to do with how students navigated the elementary system. For example, if students had been involved in special education, ever been identified

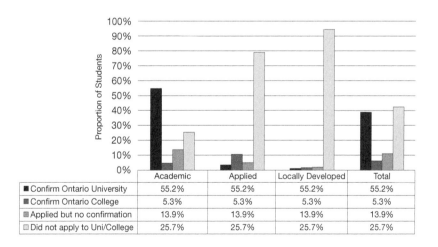

	Academic	Applied	Locally Developed	Total
■ Confirm Ontario University	55.2%	55.2%	55.2%	55.2%
■ Confirm Ontario College	5.3%	5.3%	5.3%	5.3%
▨ Applied but no confirmation	13.9%	13.9%	13.9%	13.9%
▢ Did not apply to Uni/College	25.7%	25.7%	25.7%	25.7%

Figure 5.1 Ontario Postsecondary Education Confirmations Across Program of Study, 2011–2012. Source: Parekh, 2014.

with a disability or exceptionality, ever been given an individual education plan (IEP), had modified curriculum, or had ever been placed in a special education or enrichment program, these factors can play a tremendous role in shaping students' academic pathways for high school.

Students' elementary achievement is also a major factor in their academic trajectory. However, a recent study revealed that programming often trumps achievement in terms of future access to secondary or postsecondary education. For example, in the elementary grades, students can have average to above-average achievement, yet if they are involved in special education, particularly a special education program, their access to Academic level courses in high school are highly limited (Parekh & Brown, 2019). Similarly, in high school, students in Grades 9–10 Academic who have a D in math (or a D average in their Grades 9–10 Academic-level courses) are just as likely to get into postsecondary education as students who have an A in Applied-level math (or across their Applied-level courses) (Brown et al., 2018).

Who Benefits and Who Loses?

A recent study (Archer et al., 2018) talks about the symbolic violence of setting and speaks directly to how ability-grouping marginalizes particular groups of students and how that oppression becomes embodied. Archer and colleagues (2018) claim that streaming is "counter-evidential," (p. 119) meaning it is not supported by research or empirical evidence, yet it remains an incredibly popular practice worldwide. That is because, they argue, streaming is providing another kind of service. For instance, streaming, or setting, "can be interpreted as a technology of social reproduction, which reflects the interests of the privileged and is designed to maintain social class and racialized inequalities and unequal relations" (Archer et al., 2018, p. 136).

As these authors discuss, if academic streaming were bad for everyone, it would have been scrapped eons ago. But it's not. In fact, it very much advantages a certain segment of the student population, just as it disenfranchises others. The systemic stratification of opportunity all but ensures that some students are going to be set on a trajectory of academic success with enhanced access to elite, rigorous academic programs. Just as it assures the maintenance of a working class, justi-fied through constructed underperformance and academic failure.

> *The general public acknowledges, sometimes explicitly and sometimes tacitly, that schools are this country's de facto socioeconomic sorting mechanism. Under this logic, schools are the primary place where eco-nomic futures are cast and people are sorted into their roles in society (Anyon, 1981; Carnoy & Levin, 1985; Finn 1999). In short, some people must fill the least desirable places in society, and it is important that they feel they deserve to be in those positions or, at the very least, that there is a formal mechanism to justify their place there (Bowles & Gintis, 1976; MacLoed, 1987).* (Duncan-Andrade & Morrell, 2008, pp. 2–3)

When we examined streaming, clear patterns emerged as to who exactly was benefiting from the system and who was not. Not surprisingly, as streaming and special education are so fundamentally connected, the sociodemographic trends visible within the special education system are essentially replicated across academic streams. For instance, male students are significantly overrepresented in lower streams. From our study, male students made up close to two thirds of the student pop-ulation taking the majority of their Grade 9–10 courses at the Locally Developed level (Parekh, 2013). Across the four largest racial groups (Black, South Asian, East Asian, and white), all groups were overrep-resented within the highest Academic stream with the exception of Black students who were 2 to 2.5 times as likely to be enrolled in lower streams such as Applied and Locally Developed. There is also a signif-icant discrepancy of family income across academic streams. Students in lower streams are far more likely to come from lower income families compared to students in enriched or Academic streams (Parekh, 2014).

When we spoke to students about their experiences of streaming, many addressed the issue of race and racism as being a factor in the guidance they received to select non-Academic level courses in high school. When asked whether students had noticed any demographic trend in terms of who was pursuing Academic-level courses compared to Applied, many students we interviewed noted that Black students in their school made up a large proportion of students in Applied-level programming.

Although streaming is often positioned as a choice, the implicit message is that if you are recommended or advised to pursue a non-Academic program, it is because whoever is guiding you believes you either cannot do the work or you do not belong in Academic-level courses. In discussions around perceptions of ability and expectations, two racialized students shared that when they were in Grade 8, they had both exercised their student choice to pursue an Academic program in Grade 9. But once they arrived at high school and began their courses, they soon realized that someone else had switched their timetables and had placed them in Applied-level courses. They detailed what it took to eventually switch streams so that they would have an option to pursue postsecondary education, something they both aspired to do. They also expressed that shifting streams was challenging and only made possible by educators encouraging and supporting them through the process.

Another racialized student described how they were encouraged to pursue an Applied program in high school because it was "easier," and their teacher felt they were better "suited" for an Applied pathway. The student also shared that, not once, were they informed about the implications of an Applied pathway and how unlikely it would be for them to access university later on. In fact, this student had to take it upon themselves to advocate and later demand to be moved into Academic-level courses, but the process to transfer took weeks and the student felt that they were disadvantaged by the delay.

Many educators brought up the issue of how, within the current system, students are expected to know by age 13 years what they will want to pursue after high school. As such, the educators we interviewed largely thought that delaying pathway choice made a lot of sense. The stakes are high for young students, and decisions that essentially close off postsecondary pathways should not have to be made in middle school. I was curious as to what degree students understood the implications of their course selections. But when we asked them, many students either did not know the implications of the courses they were taking or shared that they had found out too late.

The school district I have had the opportunity to work with has had a clear mandate on addressing the issue of streaming. But as one astute high school student shared, unless special education is "fixed" there is no point in "fixing" Applied. In their opinion, special education is the primary feeder into the Applied stream—they're right. As students acknowledged, to address equity in academic outcomes, the work needs to begin long before they reach high school, and it needs to address more than simply what courses are available to students in Grade 9.

Different Notions on Ability, but Ableism Still Driving Special Education and Streaming Systems

Even though streaming is an ability-based response to students' presumed ability, there is a distinct shift in language between how streaming and special education are discussed. Again, special education practices are more likely to be tied to legislation, whereas streaming is a bit more subjectively organized. Within many districts, special education is predominantly an elementary-level phenomenon. Certainly, special education programs exist at the secondary level, some support students into adulthood (often until the age of 21 or 22). However, secondary special education programs (at least in Ontario) are not nearly as popular as they are in the elementary panel. It could be argued that the reason the proportion of students enrolled in special education programs tends to drop off at the start of high school is because that is precisely the moment when the streaming system takes over and streamlines students into different ability-based pathways. Although both special education and streaming systems perform similar functions, in that they determine which students access which types of ability-based programs, the programs themselves, as well as the students within them, are discussed very differently.

For example, discussions involving disability and special education, particularly in the elementary grades, are largely focused on aligning support to address student need. In many cases, special education is discussed through a rights framework, urging families and educators to push for student access to services and supports they deem essential in giving students a fighting chance to excel (or survive) with the system. Intervention with the goal of rehabilitation and "catching up" to the norm are key motivations driving both families and educators to seek out and commit to special education services and programs. Special education is positioned as a strategy to "fix" what is constructed as "isn't working" or "problematic" within students (Brantlinger, 2006; Erevelles et al., 2006).

Although lower streams in high school (e.g., Locally Developed and Applied-level courses in our example) are predominantly enrolled by students with a history of special education programming or supports, the discourses around streaming are vastly different from those around special education in the earlier grades. Once students transition from Grade 8 into high school, an entirely different metric through which students' ability and potential are measured seems to come into play. Instead of thinking about students as arriving to school requiring intervention through services and supports, streaming students is perceived as a strategy to, instead, compensate for students' poor work ethic, behavior, and inability to apply themselves effectively. What goes unacknowledged is that, in most cases, these are the exact same students. When we track students from their days in special education, we often find them sitting in non-Academic classrooms in high school. The same kids who special education sought to save in elementary are often constructed as troublesome and disengaged when they transition into secondary.

Connection to Special Education

Having asked to speak to students who had pursued Applied level programs, just about every student we interviewed had arrived to high school with a history of special education in their elementary years. Interestingly, when asked to describe their trajectory through school and why they did not end up pursuing an Academic-level program, many students connected back to their experience in special education. Several of the students we spoke with questioned whether their involvement in special education, early on, had set them up for failure. Students shared that, in special education, they did not receive the instruction they knew their peers were receiving nor did they feel that anyone within the school held high expectations for their achievement. Students also spoke to how their removal from their general education class to attend special education programming was confusing, particularly when they were assigned work that was clearly grades behind their homeroom peers. Students felt special education was easy and that the low expectations they encountered made them feel as though no one cared whether they would be academically successful or not.

Being recommended for non-Academic programming in high school seemed to be a clear verdict on students' potential and indication of how much effort the school was willing to put into salvaging their education. From students' perspective, lower streaming was often perceived as a judgment and punishment, a solidification of low expectations and devaluation. Students shared that Applied-level programming was boring and stigmatizing and that the stigma they felt in Applied-level classrooms might also be experienced by their Applied-level teachers. It was clear to them that no one, teachers and students alike, wanted to be there.

Expectations and Care

In education, we often talk about expectations and the role expectations play in our students' success. Research shows that low expectations run rampant in special education programs (Mitchell, 2015) while expectations for students in enriched or gifted programs are much higher. What I did not understand before working with youth on expectations and programming is that, to students, expectations are also interpreted as and indicative of how much educators care. Even though high schoolers can present or posture as independent and interested in priorities outside of school, they really care that you, as their educator, care about them and believe they can be successful. In our interviews with high school students, we were repeatedly surprised by how often they invoked the concept of care and how they tied their notion of 'care' or 'of being cared for' to programming.

For example, one Grade 12 student made the connection between care, perceived ability, and inclusion. They suggested that when students are not perceived to be learning like everyone else, they are quickly excluded from the classroom. In their opinion, exclusions in school were one of the primary reasons youth ended up on the "streets," or drop out and look for work instead of pursuing postsecondary education. This student felt that it was easier for school staff to give up on students in the Applied-level program. They noted that to be successful in school you have to approach schooling and "think" like educators. If you are unable to emulate your teachers' way of thinking, the student shared that it was difficult to develop a relationship with them. In speaking with our interviewees, it seemed clear that students' ability to connect with their teachers was extremely important to them and to their well-being in school. Additionally, students' did not perceive exclusion based on ability (e.g., special education, lower streams) as remedial or necessary to support their learning, but was instead interpreted as a withdrawal or lack of care. When youth were placed in conditions that were not compatible with care, for example, being immersed in low expectations, feeling pushed out or excluded, being reminded that they do not measure up, they took this to heart and it hurt.

Streaming and Behavior

The experience of exclusion through programming can, for some students, elicit a behavioral response. Behavior is a form of communication (Lawrence-Brown et al., 2014; Killoran, 2012, personal communication). Students may not be able to articulate their experience, but they can show it to you through their behavioral response. Interestingly, we visited several high schools that were attempting to de-stream some of their Grade 9 courses, collapsing Academic and Applied level courses, and asked educators how their de-streamed or inclusive classes ran in comparison to when students were separated into Academic and Applied. We encountered an important theme: across almost all educators we interviewed, behavior was one of the biggest observed differences between the two streams. Educators we interviewed noted that students in Applied had typically been together since the early grades (a nod at the extensive streaming that takes place before secondary school) and, with a history of low expectations, generally "fool around" in class. But when they are integrated into classes with students who have experienced school differently and have always faced high expectations for learning, the students who would have been bottom streamed quickly adapted to the new conditions. Before de-streaming, behavior management was a significant component of educators' work, particularly in Applied classes, but with de-streaming that had all but disappeared.

Educators suggested that concerns around behavior have been tempered based on integrating with higher achieving students, a finding also supported through research (Mitchell, 2015). However, I query how removing the exclusionary experience of streaming from the lives of students may also play a role in decreasing students' disruptive behavioral responses in the classroom. Collapsing streams means that students are now more likely to be in educational environments that hold higher expectations for their learning—expectations that, as discussed, students read as "care." Additionally, many students spoke about how being excluded from the general education classroom led to low self-esteem, bullying, and exclusion by their peers. I think back to the anecdote my daughter shared in Grade 3. It is almost as though the system sets the example of who is valued and deserving of care—and students witness and replicate what they observe.

Interviewees also acknowledged that students in Applied classrooms were often noisier and rowdier than students in Academic; they suggested this was a "if they don't care, why should I?" kind of response to lowered expectations. However, they were also aware that others viewed this behavior as a moral failing rather than as resistance. One educator commented that all the students in Applied hung out together, toured around the school together, and that their collective behavior was known within and beyond the school. So when the school began talking about collapsing academic streams, parents expressed a great deal of concern around having "those" kids mixed in with "their" kids. Many such parents began pressuring the school to offer more enriched courses, so that their kids could leave those kids in Academic and pursue more-rigorous academic learning with a more homogenous or "like-minded" group of youth.

Note that "like-minded" is often code for racial, class, and ability homogeneity and is often evoked by proponents of academic segregation who argue that somehow taking classes with only like-minded students is to their benefit. But it is not. Several educators we interviewed suggested that working with presumably "like-minded" students actually produced a drought of innovation within the classroom. They argued that successful engagement in learning required a diversity of approaches and perspectives or else both teaching and learning became stagnant. In many ways, I interpret the term like-minded as "protectionist of privilege," particularly as it is generally argued to protect predominantly white, wealthier spaces, from which racialized students, students of a diversity of cultures, identities and communities, are excluded. When we draw on the work of Leonardo & Broderick (2011) and Mansfield (2015), it becomes clear that the fear of "mixing minds" at school draws from white supremacy and the fear of engaging in spaces where whiteness is not as overtly privileged. These structural segregations may be coded as supporting students' interests in enriched, Academic, or Applied level courses, but students read their placement in lower streamed courses as exclusion from more privileged spaces. Once students experienced exclusion in school or sensed they were being negatively judged by others, they carried that sense of exclusion with them into all facets of their lives (also see Rix & Ingham, 2021).

Between-School Streaming

Streaming does not only occur within a school. In fact, streaming between schools is also a significant issue. A macroexamination of streaming revealed inequity across systems, where schools in wealthier neighborhoods typically hosted more elite, both socially and academically valued program opportunities than did those in lower income neighborhoods. Conversely, schools in lower income neighborhoods were generally more likely to host trades, vocational, and special education programs (Parekh et al., 2011). In a study conducted in 2009, we uncovered that, within a large Ontario urban district, some community high schools within lower-income neighborhoods did not offer enough advanced course credits for students to be eligible for university admission following high school.

As researchers, we have been able to closely examine the progression of students through the education system from kindergarten to and, in some cases, through postsecondary education. Yet even within a public education system, academic streaming is complicated by factors such as school-type, program-type, and neighborhood location. Additionally, factors such as access to resources, fund-raising capacities, histories of surveillance and police presence, all inform and complicate academic streaming. For instance, in many districts, there may be an option for families to enroll their children across a choice of public high schools. Likely, one of the high schools within a student's catchment area will have a reputation for being more academic and will offer extra academic course/program options. Conversely, there will likely be a high school that has a reputation for being lower performing; it may offer more trades-focused courses and vocational training. Despite the shared neighborhood boundaries, these schools will not only exhibit academic stratification, but due to how ableism intersects with and can enact racism and class discrimination, will also often be stratified by race and class. Again, where students "end up" for high school is largely determined before students enter high school, and is influenced by their experiences and placement in elementary schools or programs (e.g., special education, gifted, elite arts, sports programs) (Gaztambide & Parekh, 2017).

Questions for Further Thought and Reflection

1. In your system, where does streaming begin? What factors play the biggest role in determining which students are streamed?
2. How does your education system prepare students for the outcomes of streaming? Are families made aware of the implications of streaming? Are students? Are educators?
3. What opportunities or supports does your school system offer students who are attempting to switch streams?

4. Despite the clear connection between elementary special education and secondary streaming, the role of families and advocacy
   can diminish once students enter secondary school. In what ways
   does your school enable entry points for families and students to
   advocate for greater support?

6

Implicating Gifted and Talented Education

"A substantial part of the ideological work of schooling constructs and constitutes some students as 'smart,' while simultaneously constructing and constituting other students as 'not-so-smart'—that is, some students are taught their intellectual supremacy and concomitant entitlement to cultural capital, whereas others are taught their intellectual inferiority and concomitant lack of entitlement to both an identity as a 'smart' person, and the cultural and material spoils that such an identity generally affords."
—LEONARDO & BRODERICK, 2011, 2014

If ableism is the privileging of ability, then it makes sense to include a discussion on the construction and social value of giftedness. As ableist systems disenfranchise historically marginalized groups through the construction of inability or disability, they also privilege individuals who are perceived to demonstrate smartness or talent. Therefore, if we are going to challenge how we traditionally think about ability, notions of giftedness and talent deserve to be integral parts of the discussion. How giftedness is addressed across jurisdictions differs dramatically. In Ontario, giftedness is a designated special education exceptionality category. Just like other special education designations, students identified as gifted in the Ontario public education system are entitled to an IEP and may be offered placement in a self-contained gifted program. This is likely a unique configuration of identification and services, but it further justifies the review of giftedness as part of discussions on ability, ableism, and ability-based hierarchies.

Historical and Current Notions of Giftedness

Much like historical notions of intelligence, giftedness is largely conceived to be biological or innate. Terman, who introduced the Stanford-Binet Intelligence Scale in 1916 (Stoeger, 2009), was dubbed the "father of gifted education" (Warne, 2019). His aim was to challenge preconceived notions around giftedness and the comorbidity with less desired physical, psychological, and emotional traits. Terman's study revealed that, on the contrary, children identified as gifted were likely to be advantaged in many other ways as well, not just in better states of health with access to social opportunities, but they also often went on to have great careers (Stoeger, 2009). However, this study was widely criticized, for its sample selection and questionable conclusions derived from insufficient data (Stoger, 2009). Although there continues to be much attention to Terman's work, it is difficult to overlook the racist and eugenic leanings that influenced his research (for more see Terman, 1916). Racism, xenophobia, sexism, and classism were evident throughout Terman's writing and notions of a social order, in which, according to Terman, white men held supremacy (Warne, 2019). Yet many of Terman's recommended practices and ideas about children, their capacity, and worth are still part of the fabric of public education today.

Currently, giftedness is assumed to be something children are born with or inherit from their parents, something confirmed through the use of psychometric testing (Gaztambide-Fernández et al., 2013). In some districts, having a gifted identification can grant students access to gifted education. Gifted education can be organized in a variety of ways, from full-day, full-time self-contained or once-a-week gifted programming, to different forms of enrichment opportunities. Some studies show limited, mixed and inequitably distributed effects on students' achievement as a result of ability-grouping and congregating students identified as gifted together (see Bui et al., 2012; Redding & Grissom, 2021; Steenbergen, et al., 2016). However, scholars debate whether

observed improved outcomes are actually a result from the congregation of "like-minds" or from the high expectations and enriched programming delivered by educators in response to students' perceived
high ability (McClure, 2007; Tieso, 2003).

Giftedness and Achievement

Regardless of placement in a gifted program or a general education
program, students identified as gifted tend to do very well in school,
graduating and accessing postsecondary education at similar rates
(Brown & Parekh, 2010). In discussions on giftedness, my colleagues
and I have been repeatedly told that we should not be conflating giftedness with current levels of achievement. Instead, we should recognize
giftedness as the identification of *potential* for future achievement and
innovation. But even the relationship between giftedness and potential is tenuous. Gladwell (2006) once shared his own experience of
being a young track star, who, contrary to the expectations of many
in his youth, became, what he described as, an average adult runner.
Gladwell (2006) spoke to the mythical assumption that children who
demonstrate notable potential in their youth will go on to yield notable
productivity and performance in their adult lives. As Gladwell (2006)
points out, to realize the potential they have been ascribed, youth must
be able to transform what they know into what they do. Yet the active
component of doing, producing, or accomplishing cannot be captured
through psychometric testing.

In many districts in Ontario, gifted identifications happen around
Grade 3 or 4 (Brown & Parekh, 2010). To explore this idea that potential can be identified early and realized later on, our research team
opted to examine whether students identified as gifted in early elementary were among the very high achievers at the end of high school
(Grade 12). Interestingly, our results showed that there was almost no
relationship between gifted identification in elementary and very high
achievement at the end of students' secondary schooling.

In terms of individuals who were identified as gifted and those who
were among the highest achievers in school, we found that they were
largely two separate groups. Students identified as gifted in the elementary years were most likely to be white, wealthy, male students, yet

the highest achievers at the end of high school were more likely to be female and identify as East, South, and Southeast Asian (for more see Parekh, Brown, & Robson, 2018).

Gifting Giftedness to a Select Few

When I began my role as a district researcher, gifted assessments were offered free of charge through the school system (although many parents paid the significant expense to have them conducted privately), and the evaluations were typically initiated by teacher referral. This meant that unless parents pushed for a gifted referral, only children whose teachers believed they had potential for giftedness would be referred for further follow-up. As we have seen from discussions in earlier chapters, impressions of students' ability can be shaped by students' sociodemographic characteristics, which can unfairly diminish the perception educators' hold around students' ability. As such, racialized students and students from lower income families are at greater risk of being overlooked for gifted referrals. Interestingly, new research is showing how racial disproportionality is reduced when the teacher making the referrals is themself racialized (Barshay, 2016). Also interestingly, girls tend to achieve at higher rates than boys across almost all measurable indicators from kindergarten to postsecondary, sharing some parity around particular measurements in mathematics (Toronto District School Board, 2015). Yet girls are disproportionately underrepresented in gifted referrals, identification, and programs (Brown & Parekh, 2010). One could argue that girls have been historically socialized to be compliant, to work hard, and to perform well in school—so their performance may not trigger the same question around brilliance as when boys perform similarly. Additionally, boys are more likely to be socialized to engage in externalizing behavior that may trigger an assessment for impairment only to uncover that they also meet the criteria for giftedness.

One of the most popular critiques of giftedness identification and subsequent programming is around the relationship to the identification of giftedness with other forms of privilege. "Researchers within the field of gifted and talented education have struggled to account for the fact that most students who benefit from gifted education programs are already advantaged by social positions and privileges"

(Gaztambide-Fernández et al., 2013, p. 125). For instance, study after study has shown that students who are white, wealthy, and enjoy other forms of privilege are more likely to be identified as gifted and, subsequently, offered gifted placements (Parekh, Brown & Robson, 2018). The relationship between whiteness and giftedness is so strong that they can become conceptually conflated (Leonardo & Broderick, 2011), similar to how the notion of smartness can be bartered and exploited to further advantage white students (Mansfield, 2015). When our small research team looked at the data on giftedness and threw other sociodemographic characteristics into the mix, white male students whose parents had high status positions were found to be the most likely combination of characteristics leading to an identification of giftedness (Parekh, et al., 2018). In many cases, the measurement of giftedness is presented as an objective, pseudo-scientific metric that measures the innate, yet it cannot seem to reconcile its relationship to social and material privilege.

In Chapter 2, we critically reviewed the roots of psychometric testing and its use as a tool to maintain white supremacy. Therefore, we should not be surprised by the exclusions these tests continue to perpetuate. And if we know that students' responses to measures within gifted evaluations are highly related to students' access to resources and opportunities, then what exactly are we testing? Either giftedness is innate, as those early gifted scholars' suggested, or it is produced through students' privilege and access, putting it at odds with its historical construction and complicating our current response to it.

Talent and Specialty Programming

Gifted programming is certainly not the only space in which advantages are afforded certain students and their families. Like special education, the streaming system has become more diffuse and difficult to trace. Rarely in discussions of streaming are elite specialty programs raised as a significant contributing factor. Their exemption from many equity analyses related to programming has allowed, in many districts, an entire specialized system to proliferate advantaging already-advantaged students. A great example of this are elite specialty arts programs. Sure, students pursuing a performance arts education likely have an interest in art and performance. But so do a lot of other kids who will never make the cut or be able to access these competitive programs. Most of the specialty arts programs in our district had or continue to have extensive entrance requirements.

Both my children love music, as many kids do, and years ago, they were both recommended by teachers to pursue a specialty arts program in musical theater performance. I figured I should probably check it out. Crammed into a hot, standing-room-only school gymnasium, I, along with all the other curious parents, listened to the specialty arts program presentation. In it, there was considerable emphasis on equity, suggesting that really, any of us attending that night had an equal chance of having our children snapped up and admitted into this elite program. That was until there was a soft recommendation to parents of any child involved in special education that they really need not bother applying. It was claimed that the academic program at the school was so rigorous, there would be little capacity on the part of the school to support or accommodate.

Following more talk on the application process and emphasizing how they are really looking for children who have a passion for performing arts, they noted that for admissions it would be a great asset if the child had also reached a particular level in piano as determined through Royal Conservatory of Music. It was clear that equity-in-access was only applicable to nondisabled students and families wealthy enough to afford classical piano music lessons for their child. This program was entirely coded as catering to the interests of passionate, young performing artists committed to honing their artistic craft, while at the same, explicitly excluding students on the basis of disability and class. I have come to understand that these exclusionary policies have since been amended, but sometimes policies do not have to be on the books to be built into the fabric of an institution.

As a postdoctoral fellow, I had the opportunity to write with a leading scholar on elite schooling, Dr. Rubén Gaztambide-Fernández. Building on his extensive scholarship in the field, we explored the pathways and demographic composition of specialty arts programs (Gaztambide-Fernández & Parekh, 2017). At the time, specialty arts programs were hosted by four public high schools throughout the district and admissions were highly sought after. Students had to undertake portfolio submissions or auditions to be granted acceptance. These programs also received enhanced funding to support their programming needs. Our study found that although placement in specialty arts programs were open to students across the district, the bulk of students granted admission came from a select few feeder schools. Additionally, the students accessing specialty arts programs were notably white and wealthy. Although the focus of specialty arts programs was on the arts, students attending these programs may not have had any interest in pursuing a career in the arts. In some cases, "the arts are construed as playing a role in a holistic education that prepares students for university and for careers as lawyers, doctors, and architects" (Gaztambide-Fernández, 2013, p. 223). Through the admissions process, students admitted into specialty arts programs have proven themselves to be gifted and/or talented and can use their admission as evidence or justification that they have met a particular threshold of excellence that can be applied to other vocations (Gaztambide-Fernández, et al., 2013).

At one time, our district opened up a slew of specialized schools. One specialized school was focused on vocal performance and it was ensured that the school would be highly accessible to anyone who had an interest in performance—no fees or audition necessary. What happened? Very few students came and the program faced an uncertain future (Brown, 2016). So when systems set up specialized programming catering to notions of brilliance or talent, their draw may not really be about the substance of the program, but more about the confirmation of excellence these programs provide (Gaztambide-Fernández et al., 2013).

According to our data, programs that cater to students demonstrating "excellence" are disproportionately occupied by wealthy white and East Asian students. The environment fostered in gifted and talented programs generally comes with high expectations for student potential and focuses on innovation, skill development, and opportunities to pursue interesting and often stimulating academic work. Lost in all of the positive attributes that elite programs offer is the fact that they are very much contributing to the stratification and ability-based hierarchy of students. Inclusion, and its benefits for lower-performing students, is typically acknowledged as a key equity strategy. However, inclusion as it relates to elite programming, is more likely to be described as a loss, as something being taken away from deserving (as defined by ability) children. In fact, educators reported that schools who were attempting to be more inclusive were losing families to other schools offering more elite, specialized programs. They shared that should their school give up their enriched programming, they would experience a significant drop in enrolment.

How Do Notions of Giftedness and Talent Shape our Understanding of Disability?

The identification and attention to giftedness and talent have only exacerbated the marginalization of disabled children within education. While we can discuss how ability is constructed, children and their families live out the consequences of these constructions. As an example, I was once asked to speak at a conference about a recent study I had conducted on students' experience of belonging and exclusion in school. For my doctoral thesis, I had created a measure of belonging that was intended to mirror the literature on social citizenship and capture students' experience of safety, acceptance from peers and educators, and shared power within the classroom and school (for more see Parekh, 2014). For whatever reason, a significant proportion of my parent audience was there on behalf of their children who were identified as gifted.

The results of my study, based on the accounts of thousands of children, provided further evidence of a strong relationship between how students are organized by ability and the subsequent exclusion disabled students face. Students organized into less socially valued programs reported significantly higher levels of exclusion coupled with precarious post–high school pathways. I found the data damning and was hoping for allyship among the audience in recognizing how the practices of organizing students by ability were detrimental to the well-being of students.

When I paused for questions, the first comment I received was one of thanks for finally providing evidence that congregating students by ability worked. Confused, I tried to reexplain the findings. The attendee persisted and suggested that I look more closely at my own data regarding students in gifted programming as they reported the highest level of "belonging." In their view, that particular data point reaffirmed that gifted programming worked and that it was clearly best for, as they described, brilliant "like minds" to not have to navigate the masses, but instead to only have to work alongside their intellectual equals. I pointed to the significant exclusion experienced by students in special education programs and schools, and reiterated how these programs and their ideologies are interrelated, and that the privileging of some meant the disenfranchisement of others. The attendee was unmoved and asked for a copy of my slides.

The follow-up question was from another attendee who shared that they were struggling with their child who had been identified as gifted. They were reportedly having a hard time making friends in school because they were so much "better" than their peers who were struggling to overcome their jealousy. I do not recall any other questions that followed. After all the work system and advocacy groups had been doing around the issue of equity and social justice, the ranking of children by ability and assigning human value to that ranking continued to be normalized. This is why the work of disability justice needs to push not only for a reconceptualization of disability but also for a resistance to notions of all forms of ability tethered to human value. We need to continue the work on disentangling ability from whiteness, ableism from white supremacy, and challenge how ability is used to define or determine human value.

Questions for Further Thought and Reflection

Enrichment opportunities inherently create conditions through which ability is privileged. But because enrichment opportunities are typically framed as opportunities for students to pursue their interests, the discussion around what to do with enrichment programs in the context of inclusion can be tricky.

With your school or school experiences in mind, think through the following:

1. What types of admission processes are required for your school's enrichment programs? Which students do those requirements include? Exclude? What values do they promote?
2. When you think about who ends up accessing enrichment programs, what types of trends do you observe in terms of racial, class, and disability demographics?
3. When you envision your school's approach to inclusion, how are enrichment opportunities discussed in the context of equity?

Part III

Practical Strategies for the School and Classroom

7

Critical Approaches to Inclusion

"This means developing radical inclusive pedagogy that
abandons the pursuit of norms and standards in favour of
supporting children to better understand themselves, the
world and their relations with others in the world, while
taking into account the full range of human embodiments
and support needs"

—GREENSTEIN, 2016, P. 5

We have thus far explored critical perspectives on special education and academic streaming and are left with questions as to what we can do to challenge ableism in our work and relationships with students. Intuitively, inclusion seems to be the answer to historically exclusionary policies and practices. But what is inclusion? What does inclusion mean and how can it be implemented, particularly when approached from a disability studies in education (DSE) perspective?

When I first started teaching in Faculties of Education, I used to run field trips to our local district's Special Education Advisory Committee (SEAC) meetings. In the US, IDEA "requires that each State establish and maintain an advisory panel for the purpose of advising the State special education staff regarding the education of eligible children with disabilities" (State of Nevada Department of Education, n.d.). In Ontario, every public board of education is required to have a SEAC to support the district's understanding of special education and implementation of special education services (O. Reg. 464/97 under Education Act, R.S.O. 1990, c. E.2.). Their meetings are public and anyone can attend. A number of disability organizations and groups supporting children identified through special education have representatives that sit on their local SEAC committees. As a collective, SEAC can develop and forward recommendations to the district around their special education priorities and practices. As my classes generally focused on disability theory and disability studies in education, attending a SEAC meeting enabled graduate students to see theory in practice. SEAC representatives often approached special education from a perspective that reflected the values of their organizations. Some were in favor of more-inclusive approaches, where some were advocating for an expansion of self-contained special education programming. All were there to represent the interests and priorities of the communities they served. Even though we could discuss theoretical notions of disability and emancipatory approaches to education in our classroom, it was important to me that my students experience what it is like to have several perspectives about disability converge for the purpose of collectively making recommendations to the system. Because, rarely, will you find yourself in a room where everyone agrees.

The first meeting our class attended ran through the committee's typical business items but, to our surprise, the bulk of the time together was spent discussing what inclusion really means and would look like in schools. Of course, advocates asserted that inclusion is a right enshrined in the Convention on the Rights of Persons with Disabilities, but it was argued that the imposition of inclusion conflicted with the parents' choice for specialized education, primarily, gifted education. It was brought up that research generally supported inclusion, yet many times those studies failed to detail what was meant by inclusion beyond integration, and even then, the context and extent of integration was sometimes fuzzy. After an hour of intense and, at times, heated exchanges of ideas, there was still no consensus reached. In fact, the discussion closed with representatives visibly upset that they had not been able to further sway the committee in one direction or another.

While leaving the meeting, a number of my students and I jumped on public transit to make our way home. We took the opportunity to unpack what we had observed. Students shared that they could clearly recognize the challenge of effecting any kind of system change when disability and equity was approached from such a diversity of perspectives. Those arguing for the adoption of a social justice perspective on disability and greater inclusion came into direct conflict with those who perceived equity for disabled students as expanding special education programming. As such, the committee was perceived to be deadlocked and, therefore, struggled to make recommendations, either way, to the district. But students identified three key omissions from the discussions they had witnessed.

1. The voice of representatives advocating for the rights of children identified as gifted and learning disabled, typically connected to more affluent and privileged communities, often dominated discussions, drowning out representatives advocating for children with more stigmatized identifications and exclusionary experiences in school.

2. The representatives on the committee, for the most part, were there on behalf of the communities they served, but unlike other equity-seeking groups, many did not share the identities or experiences of the children they represented. Many representative roles were taken on by parents of disabled children, a critically important perspective to include, but the recommendations around special education were generally not informed by people with lived experience of disability.

3. One astute student also noted that while the committee discussed what inclusion should look like, who should be included, and to what extent they should be included, it was never brought up exactly what students were being included into. What would be required of general classroom environments to ensure the inclusion of disabled students is safe and honoring? If ableist values and assumptions around capacity are baked into the very fabric of schooling, how will that be appropriately addressed in general education so as not to socially or psychically exclude within an "inclusive" model of education?

Recognizing how difficult it was for the school district to land on a concept of inclusion, in 2015, my colleague, Dr. Kathryn Underwood, and I wrote a short piece in an attempt to lay out what inclusion *is* and *is not* (the italicized components of the following sections are directly drawn from Parekh & Underwood, 2015, pp. 4–5).

What Is Inclusive Education?

An inclusive classroom is a place where all students experience a sense of belonging and social citizenship (e.g., membership, inclusion, shared power, and value) (Parekh, 2014). Years earlier, I conducted quite a bit of research on students' experience of belonging in school. Belonging was not only tied to student achievement, but was also tied to identity and programming. Students who were identified through special education or were placed in special education programming reported heightened experiences of exclusion. This finding, to me, spoke to the inhospitable conditions of schooling disabled students face including how an identification of disability or exceptionality (excluding gifted) through special education immediately places students in conflict with the tenets and goals of schooling. In inclusive classrooms, educators intentionally challenge ableism to create both safe and welcoming spaces.

An inclusive classroom modifies the environment to fit the student, not the student to fit the environment. If students are struggling, the first step is to examine and adjust the environment to determine whether there could be hidden barriers within the classroom. Ask students; many will be able to help you uncover what they find distracting or what might be preventing them from engaging in or completing their work. Assessment is a key component of inclusion. Every time educators make changes to the environment, it is helpful to reach back to students to check in as to how that adjustment may or may not have made a difference.

An inclusive classroom is a space where all identities and cultures (including disability culture) are celebrated. As discussed with culturally relevant and responsive pedagogy, inclusive classrooms uphold principles of justice for all identities, cultures, and communities within the class. Attention, representation, and inclusion of disability culture is important.

An inclusive classroom prioritizes the right to participation and focuses on setting a positive climate where social engagement and friendships can be promoted (Underwood, 2013). There is a TEDx Talk by Dan Habib

(2014) on inclusion called *Disabling Segregation*. In it, he asks the audience (I am paraphrasing here), what played a bigger role in who they were as people today—their social experiences or their academic experiences in school. The majority of the audience responded that it was their social experiences that had a larger influence over who they grew up to be. Prioritizing the right to participation, positive classroom climate and the promotion of friendships will help support students' social experiences in school.

An inclusive classroom rejects deficit thinking and does not segregate or organize students according to ability. The organization of students by ability is not only in reference to special education and inclusive classrooms but also refers to educators' current practices as they relate to organizing students by ability within the classroom. For example, how are students acknowledged in the class, who is given leadership positions, and how are rewards allocated? Modeling language that values students and rejecting deficit language are effective strategies to reorient deficit thinking.

What Inclusive Education Is Not

Inclusion is not assimilation (Slee, 2009). *The goal of inclusion is not to normalize students or create sameness within a classroom. Inclusive education celebrates diversity and creates a space where all students with disabilities can feel a sense of pride.* This means that classrooms normalize and respond to difference and integrate material, language, and ties to curriculum that are reflective of and responsive to students' experiences, knowledges, and histories.

Inclusive education does not restrict opportunities and spaces where students with disabilities can be together. Students with disabilities should have the opportunity to meet, and to create networks and communities of support. This point will be discussed further in the final chapter of this book, but what might these spaces look like? I recently came across a poster that was advertising many student-led advocacy groups taking place within schools. There were groups challenging anti-Black racism, promoting gay–straight alliances, groups supporting and welcoming new immigrants to Canada, all student led, all offering community and opportunities to share experiences and strategize. What could a disability-centered, youth-led group look like? What kind of opportunities for community and political organization might that offer disabled students?

Inclusive education is not drawn from a template; there is no one-size-fits-all formula. Inclusive schools and classrooms are organized and responsive to the demographics of students in attendance (Artiles et al., 2011). The makeup of a classroom can change from year to year or, depending on what might be occurring within the school or within broader society, the classroom dynamics and students' lives can change in an instant. Therefore, inclusion is never finalized; there is no point at which inclusion is definitively reached. As such, educators must constantly be thinking of how best to respond to the students in the classroom.

Inclusive education is not static; there is no end point where the inclusive education project is complete. Inclusive education is a continual state of becoming. It is a project that requires continuous review, assessment, and revision (Artiles et al., 2011). To practice inclusion means to be ever-assessing, reflecting on, and revising one's own practice. In addition to promoting greater equity, inclusion resists stagnancy in practice and enables educators to be creative and innovative as well as to inspire creativity and innovation in their students.

Using a Disability Studies in Education Approach to Supporting Students, Educators, and Families

Inclusive education is a way to promote greater equity for disabled students in school. However, approaching inclusion from a DSE perspective requires schools to adopt a critical vision of inclusion that goes beyond placing students together in a classroom. The dismantling of exclusionary practices and the challenge to extinguish deficit constructions of ability are coupled with the reconceptualization of disability as identity and disability justice. These perspectives and activities offer many opportunities for students, educators, and families to engage in and support the disability movement.

Thinking Critically About Disability With Students

A critical approach to disability offers students an opportunity to explore disability from, what might be for most, a novel perspective. Disability conceived as both *produced experience* and *celebrated identity* resists the dominant deficit narrative typically perpetuated in public education. Introducing topics like disability culture, disability identity, and disability rights can be liberating for many students who have grown up through an ableist education system. DSE offers students new language, new ideas, and new ways to identify ableism within their experiences both inside and outside of school. Thinking about disability using a DSE template can also support students when talking to their families about disability and help their families adopt language and concepts that honor disability. When DSE principles are integrated into classrooms, it enables students to be aware of ableism in popular language and expressions. Resisting and challenging the use of popular language that is derogatory toward disability is another way that students can promote disability justice within their own spheres of influence and engagement.

Books and film can be powerful mediums to use with students to explore ableism and disability discrimination. Through popular novels and film, students can explore topics such as how disability is portrayed in both historical and futuristic worlds, how disability might be used as a vice to represent innocence, criminality, or villainous characters. Novels and film are also useful in examining how madness and disability are represented through the context of race and gender and how disabled lives are valued. Literature and film offer opportunities to more safely engage with challenging notions that touch us all, and can, at the same time, sharpen students' critical analytic skills.

Most of all, working with children on DSE can enhance their critical consciousness and help them contribute to ideas, discussions, and actions that are socially just. For me, learning about DSE was like suddenly being able to make sense of my own life experiences as a youth, a student, and an educator. I think we underestimate the shame and blame students experience in our schools and the embodiment of ableism. DSE represents promise, a radical reorientation for how disability can be addressed in schools, and a resistance of ableist institutional values. Approaching disability through a DSE lens lets students know that regardless of how they engage, how they demonstrate their learning, and how they share and produce knowledge, their contributions are valued.

Thinking Critically About Disability With Families

When it comes to the education of children, parents are powerful partners and allies. Families are deeply invested in the welfare of their children and hold limitless aspirations for their children's futures. Unequivocally, families are willing to make economic, social, and health sacrifices to support their children through the schooling system. Families are also quick studies of their child(ren)'s school dynamics and may request or demand change if they feel that their children are entering classrooms in which they are not being academically or socially successful. When it comes to disability, it is important to recognize that families may not share the same worldview of childhood development or disability that is espoused by special education (Underwood & Parekh, 2020). Families are apt to view their child(ren) more holistically than through a narrow (often deficit-oriented) understanding on ability. Therefore, when it comes to disability, families' perspectives can be in conflict with the perspectives held by the school (Underwood, et al., 2019).

Prior to moving a student into special education, parents or caregivers are given a lot of information about what the system can offer. However, there is a lot of information families are not typically provided. For instance, families are generally *not* told that, by entering into special education programming, their child will likely experience a dramatic decrease in postsecondary opportunities. Nor are they told that, coupled with limited trajectories, their child will also likely face increased social stigma and exclusion in school. Struggling with the disconnect between what families expect and what systems provide, an administrator once suggested that selling families on the idea of a special education placement has been likened to selling *bad real estate*, where those within the system know the implications are dire, yet, special education often seems inevitable and the only intervention made available for many families and educators. To families, special education is positioned as a benevolent, supportive, and caring space; as something necessary for the *now*, regardless of the future. Rarely are families alerted to special education's history of perpetuating deficit perceptions of ability (Parekh, Brown, & Zheng, 2018); positioning children as "a problem" (Erevelles et al., 2006); or heightened experiences of bullying, and reduced opportunities to forge positive relationships (Parekh, 2014). Additionally, the offer of special education programming is often coupled with the caveat that should families choose not to pursue a special education placement, they are also choosing to forego support. As such, many families are left with the choice of support in a special education setting or no support in the general education classroom (Underwood et al., 2019).

In public education systems, families whose children appear to be struggling have been told, and sold, for generations, that special education is where they must go for help. Special education is supposed to offer the services, assessments, and programs that their children are purported to need. But over the years, studies have found little evidence to support many of the practices involved in special education (Mitchell, 2010; 2015). In fact, research has instead found that more-inclusive approaches to education typically result in either no change or significantly better social and academic outcomes (Hehir et al., 2016; Mitchell, 2014). Adopting a disability studies approach enables families to identify and advocate for targeted interventions within learning environments that also honor their child. Adopting a DSE perspective can help families hold systems accountable and position their child, and all disabled children, as rights holders.

Thinking Critically About Disability With Educators

Educators hold a privileged position in schools and in the lives of students. When working with disabled children, educators' understanding of disability is critical in fostering meaningful relationships with both students and their families. Many Faculties of Education offer courses on special education and inclusion. However, students arrive to education programs with their own understanding of ability, often informed by their own school, family and community experiences. Formative experiences related to ability can significantly shape our worldview and influence how we understand distinctions between ability, inability, and disability. Due to the prevalence of special education in public school districts, many educators went to schools where disabled children were segregated into separate programs. Unless educators have a personal connection to disability in their own lives or outside of school, their experience of learning in community with disabled people may be scant or framed through the same deficit lens they were taught through as children. Because special education presents such significant access barriers to postsecondary education (Parekh & Brown, 2019), more often than not, educators entering the school system have not, themselves, been educated through the special education system. Therefore, although all educators have their own understanding of ability, disability can seem to be a distant and unfamiliar concept. Engaging in the unfamiliar requires vulnerability, an openness to learning from others, and being prepared to shift practice. But all of this takes work and a commitment to justice.

It is critical that we also explore how teacher education programs prepare teacher candidates for working with disabled children. Even when courses are teaching about inclusion and inclusive practice, how they are taught is left up to the discretion of teacher educators. Therefore, there is no safeguard against teaching material that perpetuates notions of impairment that are heavily steeped within the medical model of disability. For example, in many special education or inclusive education focused courses, teacher candidates are taught different exceptionality types, the symptomology associated with different disorders, how to navigate special education, how to complete an individualized education plan (IEP), and how to make referrals. Rarely do teacher education programs include aspects of disability justice or expose teacher candidates to notions of disability identity, culture, or to disability history and activism. Instead, regardless of progressive instructional practice, teacher education often omits attention to more justice-centered approaches to education that have the potential to support disabled students throughout their schooling.

DSE provides educators with an alternative view of disability, one that enables educators to think about disability outside of a medical or individual model. DSE challenges educators to think about how they can integrate disability history, disabled knowledges, and disability rights into the curriculum. Adopting a DSE framework encourages educators to maximize the participation of all students and provide multiple entry points into their lessons and activities. DSE principles recognize that the expression of knowledge and demonstration of learning can take many forms, all of which have value. This framework urges educators to think about how they respond to disability and how to shape their practice in a way that values the identity and experiences of disabled students.

Questions for Further Thought and Reflection

1. Which principle of inclusion most surprised you? Which principle can you envision your school prioritizing as a school-wide goal?
2. What are some in-class strategies you can implement that both acknowledge and integrate disability identity?
3. Disability studies in education can empower educators, families, and students. What are some strategies educators can implement now that can enhance disability representation within the classroom?

8

Inclusive Pedagogy and Practice

*"Students learn in many different ways. In order for
students to be successful, educators must be flexible in their
approaches, drawing from a repertoire of methodologies that
value differentiation and support individualization"*

—CONNOR & ANNAMMA, 2014, P. 133

P racticing inclusion in the classroom is important and is a step toward real-
izing greater equity and justice in schools. However, there is no
formula for how to "do" inclusion. What works for the class you
have today will likely have to be refined for the class you have tomor-
row. Also, figuring out what works best for your classroom takes time.
As we know, teaching is relational, and unless you have the time to
get to know your students and trial a number of approaches, it can
be challenging to know which combination of strategies will be most
successful. Nevertheless, there are some strategies you can begin implementing right away.

Modeling Your Commitment to Inclusion and Justice

When you meet your students for the first time, there is a moment where
they will be sizing you up in anticipation of how the class will be run, what
kinds of hierarchies might be established, and how they will be perceived
to fit in. It is important that these first interactions intentionally demonstrate a commitment to a safe classroom space and positive classroom climate. We are asking students to engage with us and in our classes for a

number of hours a week—it is up to us to ensure these spaces are safe and supportive. These commitments can be articulated through your decisions about what types of language you use, what posters you select to put on the walls, and what material you make available within your classroom. Some classrooms begin the year with a co-constructed commitment to sustaining a respectful and socially just space—a social contract—codeveloped and signed by students and the teacher. Modeling language that respects students' identities and resists deficit thinking is critical, as is ensuring your students know that the classroom is a supportive space to explore questions around their identity and histories. It is also important to establish clear restorative interventions when the social contract is broken.

It is important that students feel safe and valued in the classroom. Students identified through special education or who identify as disabled often feel that the classroom can be a hostile and challenging environment (see Parekh, 2014). Key strategies to promote inclusion involve giving all students a chance to contribute to class discussions through various multimedia approaches. Ensuring students have the right to pass when called on and establishing that making mistakes is a welcome and necessary part of learning can create a more inclusive classroom environment. Engage students in problem solving. Integrate students' perspectives into classroom planning. Avoid using sarcasm with students. Some educators are known for their great sense of humor, which can promote a sense of camaraderie in the classroom. But sarcasm can be a subtle (or not so subtle) way of making fun.

Developing a Class Profile

Before you meet students, you will likely have access to students' records. However, these records are not always up-to-date and may be missing key information. Information in students' files can also be challenging to contextualize until you have a better sense of the students and understand their approach to learning. A quick strategy for learning what your students are bringing to the class is to ask them to complete a learning profile. (This can be done electronically using an online form or cue cards that students complete and return.)

Typically, when I begin a class, I ask students key questions such as (these can be amended):

- What are they most interested in learning over the class/year?
- What are they most concerned about in terms of expectations in the class/year?
- What goals do they have for the future?
- In what ways do they best learn? (Through group or individual work? At-home or in-class work? Types of technology students find useful?)
- What can I, as their teacher, do to better support their learning in class?
- Ask them to provide one unique fact about themselves, such as an interest they have outside of school.

Once you collect information from your students, you will be able to review collective learning strategies, goals for the future, and ways you can integrate support into your lesson planning. Asking for a unique fact can function as an anchor in remembering a student's profile and helps develop a relationship with your students. The information can also be tapped for planning future assignments and tasks.

Coteaching and Coplanning

Coplanning and coteaching are important ways schools can support educators in their practice of inclusion (European Agency for Development in Special Needs Education, 2001, 2004; Parekh, 2019). Educators do not always have a say in how their timetables are constructed. However, ensuring educators have the opportunity to coplan and coteach is important. Promoting inclusion requires thoughtful and intentional timetabling and staffing. In such decisions, it is important to factor in how educators work, who they best work with, and plan accordingly. From our interviews, educators who team-taught in inclusive classrooms often shared leadership and supportive roles. Coteaching opportunities were typically prioritized for subjects like language and mathematics, where one teacher would lead and the other would offer support to the class. Educators described this strategy as significantly enriching the classroom. Coteaching enabled educators to support the students who would have left the class for special education programming. By establishing a flexible option for in-class support, educators were also able to reach students who may be struggling but not officially identified through special education. A win-win situation!

Accommodations and Planning

From your class profile, you will see a diversity of strengths, interests, and preferred approaches to learning. Some students may share which accommodations that they find helpful to support their studies. Even if students' records do not include information from special education, every class will have students who are currently working through barriers to their learning. Many students who identify as disabled are not recognized by the special education system (Parekh & Brown, 2020). Additionally, students may be grappling with concerns around mental health, physiological conditions that may be temporary or permanent, as well as with significant life changes (e.g., death of a loved one, moving or family separation). Accommodations are key strategies that educators can put in place to support student learning. Accommodations are central to accessibility whether it be ensuring access to different components of the academic program or to the curriculum itself. They are also important in terms of assessment and evaluation. Students may require extra time to complete assignments or tests, they may benefit from access to technology or to visual cues in the classroom. When accommodations are integrated into the classroom program and targeted toward one or a small number of students (particularly if those accommodations are obvious), there is significant risk that students will refuse the accommodation. The stigma often associated with visible accommodations in school can produce a threat to students' self-identity and can prevent students from engaging with their work. Much of the work in DSE is to address the root of this stigma. Everyone needs accommodations from time to time, but only certain accommodations are stigmatized. Accommodations and normalizing the use of accommodations are critical features of an inclusive classroom. Incorporating accommodations into program design not only enables students who are formally entitled to accommodations to access without feeling singled out, but also offers key accommodations to students who may benefit even if they have not been identified through special education.

During my research in high schools, an educator shared an

excellent example of how implementation is just as, or maybe even more, important than the accommodation itself. In this scenario, a particular high school educator was responsible for the distribution of special education–funded equipment (mostly laptops) and would often pop into their students' classrooms to see how often these laptops were in use. Even during high-stakes tests or assignments, the educator reported that, most of the time, students kept their laptops in their backpacks or tucked under their desks. The educator wondered whether students' hesitancy to use their equipment might have something to do with the large security stickers adhered to each machine. These stickers indicated that the computer was purchased specially through special education. The educator also queried whether there was a social stigma in pulling out a computer during a class when you might be the only one, or one of a few, using a device. To test their theories further, the educator connected with teachers to determine their test/exam schedules and strategically placed the school's laptop cart, a complete class set of generic laptops, outside the classroom door. Additionally, the educator had asked teachers to let *all* their students know that they had an open invitation to use a laptop for a particular activity. Under these conditions, they observed that many students opted to use computers from the laptop cart, including each student who had a district-issued device. This anecdote exemplifies how access to accommodations is not necessarily synonymous with inclusion. The conditions in which accommodations are made available are just as important as ensuring students have equitable access in the classroom.

When developing plans for your class, proactive integration of accommodations can reduce significant anxiety for students. In speaking to students, asking their teacher for accommodations was one of their most challenging tasks. Students feared reprisal, lowered expectations, as well as being told "no" and denied the critical accommodations they knew they needed to be successful. Students also shared that asking for accommodations was risky because they did not want their teachers to think they did not belong in the class and be subsequently recommended to transfer to a lower level or special education. Many students identified simple accommodations that would have saved them time and the embarrassment of having to continually ask for help. Integrating accommodations into the fabric of your class design not only normalizes their use and reduces stigmatization but also lets students know what is possible and how to recognize access and inclusion in the future.

Once you learn what will benefit students in your classroom, you can integrate those accommodations into your plans. For example, if you are preparing a test and believe it should take 30 minutes to complete, but you also know that five students in your class have accommodations for extra time on tests, you can embed that extra time into your plans upfront. In this case, you can give your class 45 minutes to complete the test which will likely support the students who needed more time as well as the other students who had trouble sleeping the night before, may experience test anxiety, or students who appreciate time to review. Of course, you can still offer extra time for students should they require to complete the test, but shifting the frame of how the test is taken initially will increase inclusivity and reduce the need for students to ask for accommodations.

Another example might be that you have a very busy, well-organized day. Students received their timetables at the beginning of the year and have largely committed each day's schedule to memory. But you also know that you have a couple of students who struggle with planning. When you check in with them throughout the day, they seem less prepared to change classes and have a hard time with transition. In this case, posting a visual schedule in the classroom, perhaps posted to the class wall or taped to every student's desk could be helpful to all students in the class. When assigning a task, ensure that instructions are also available to students in multiple formats (e.g. orally, visually, etc.). Generally, the golden rule with accommodations is that what is necessary for some is likely good for all.

Modifications: A Word of Caution

Modifications are also discussed as a strategy to support students, but I would like to offer a word of caution around their usage. Modifications to curriculum expectations occur when aspects of curricular expectations are either removed or changed to support student learning. Modified curriculum could include removing curricular strands from a particular subject area. Modification can also reflect a change in the expectations around the level of mastery students are required to demonstrate in order to receive a passing grade or be granted the course credit. In Ontario, how much a secondary course can be modified and still be deemed passable can differ across jurisdictions and even within jurisdictions as decisions are at the discretion of the principal (Ontario Ministry of Education, 2017).

Modifying students' curricular expectations is often conceived as a strategy reserved for students who are believed to have intellectual exceptionalities or who have been identified as gifted. However, a recent study revealed that modified curriculum is frequently used for students following a general education program (Brown, Parekh, & Zheng, in progress). In some instances, students' curricular expectations are set to reflect a grade or two earlier (e.g., a Grade 6 student working on Grade 4 curricular expectations). Although modifying curricular expectations may appear to be an immediate solution, the consequences of modifying curriculum are long lasting. Research is showing that modifications in a curricular area result in a gap that can rarely be closed within a public education setting (Brown, Parekh & Zheng, in progress).

One of the most popular areas for modified curricular expectations is in mathematics. Modifications in mathematics often include the removal of particular curricular strands or the inclusion of earlier grade expectations. Should these modifications take place in the elementary grades, it is highly unlikely that students will be able to pursue mathematics courses in secondary school that could enable their eligibility to access postsecondary education. Modifying curriculum has heavy consequences. While unintentional, the act of modifying curriculum when students are as young as 8 and 9 years of age is likely to have implications on whether that student will have access to postsecondary education and/or economic independence as an adult. Educators must approach modifications with extreme caution and a contingency plan for how the school will intentionally address the gap created by curricular modifications. Using their professional judgment, educators might modify expectations within particular assignments or activities in class. However, modifications that limit students' future access to curriculum should be, if at all possible, avoided.

Differentiation

Luckily, educators can often avoid modifying curriculum through differentiated instruction. Underlying inclusive practice is the understanding that using the same approach for all students will not work. To maximize student engagement and access to curriculum, educators can integrate opportunities for differentiation throughout their planning and approach to activities. Adopting the principles of Universal Design for Learning (UDL) can facilitate lesson planning and classroom design. Principles of UDL ask educators to consider how to support student engagement, students' access to and representation of material, as well as how students can demonstrate their learning (Posey, n.d.).

Effective differentiated instruction adopts UDL principles. Tomlinson (2001) identified four areas that educators could differentiate: Content, process, product, and learning environment. *Content* refers to what students learn (e.g., curriculum, material available in the class) and *process* describes the methods through which educators teach and students learn (e.g., how teaching is scaffolded and how students engage with the material). The *product* refers to how students demonstrate their learning, and the *environment* refers to the learning environment. Each of these components can be differentiated in relation to students' interests, preferences, and readiness. Integrating choice and flexibility into the elements of learning will enable greater inclusion and engagement. For more information, check out Tomlinson and Imbeau's work, *Leading and Managing a Differentiated Classroom* (2010).

Direct Instruction

Direct instruction is an important part of differentiated instruction and a valuable tool for educators. Due to its conflation with didactic teaching styles, direct instruction often has an unfair reputation of being ineffective. However, research shows that, when done well, direct instruction is highly effective. According to Hattie (2009), to be effective, direct instruction has seven key components—here is a synthesis of their overview. Prior to the lesson, the educator should set clear "learning intentions" and "success criteria." Direct instruction must build engagement and orient students toward the learning task. Educators can use a variety of methods to present the lesson, but each should include a form of input (where the teacher shares information), modeling (where the teacher models the expectations for students' end product), and gauging students' understanding (checking in with students to see if they are on the right track). Direct instruction often includes a component of "guided practice" where students can show what they have learned followed by directed closure of the activity. The last component Hattie (2009) recommends is independent practice where the skill is intentionally revisited, reviewed, and rehearsed to consolidate students' learning.

> *In a nutshell: The teacher decides the learning intentions and success criteria, makes them transparent to the students, demonstrates them by modeling, evaluates if they understand what they have been told by checking for understanding, and re-telling them what they have told by tying it all together with closure (see Cooper, 2006).* (Hattie, 2009, p. 206)

Direct instruction works best when educators can also differentiate how information is shared and modeled as well as how students can demonstrate their learning.

Designing an Inclusive Activity or Assignment

Integrating the principles of differentiated instruction, maximizing choice is integral to designing an inclusive assignment or activity. As much as possible, students should have choice over different components of the assignment, noting that the demonstration of some particular skills may be nonnegotiable. For example, if the lesson is teaching students how to construct or write a paragraph, then the product should be a paragraph. However, differentiation can include offering students choice over what topic they choose to write about and options for how they write it (e.g. hand written, use of technology, speech to text software, etc.).

Examples of choice:

- Design an assignment in which students can choose which questions to respond to from a series of questions.
- Offer students the opportunity to choose which aspect of the topic students can address to demonstrate their learning.
- Include options as to what format students can select to demonstrate their understanding/learning. For example, to measure conceptual understanding of a particular topic, I might offer students the choice of writing a short paper or creating a podcast, a blog post, video essay, etc.

Designing an Inclusive Question and Entry Points to Discussions

When initiating a new activity or attempting to engage students in an activity, educators often ask a lot of questions to gauge student understanding. However, the framing of comprehension-oriented questions can immediately include or exclude students from the discussion. For example, when educators introduce a new concept, say in science, they may have students test that concept by conducting an experiment at their desks. Following the experiment, educators might ask students to speak to their results by asking them to, "Describe what happened," or "Why did that happen?" Even though students may have moved through the motions of the experiment, some may require further examples or more time to fully process or articulate the concept being demonstrated. Asking questions that require students to move through multiple conceptual processes independently and draw on new information to reach their conclusion can be overwhelming. Therefore, ensuring that all students have an entry point into the discussion is key to inclusive practice (To, 2021).

All entry points should be open and accessible. To do so, try out questions like "What did you observe?" or "What kinds of questions did the experiment/activity raise?" Instead of asking students to respond independently in front of the class, sharing first with peers in heterogenous groups can be helpful. When students contribute responses that deviate from what might be expected, find the link and reiterate how important it is to generate ideas that push boundaries. Through independent learning and group discussion, ensure students have the opportunity to amend and construct their work as they learn independently and from others (To, 2021).

Making Groups

Prioritizing group work is an important strategy in promoting inclusion. Organizing students into heterogenous groups allows for students to work and learn from each other (Parekh, 2019). As highlighted throughout this book thus far, children often learn better from other children than they do from a teacher at the front of the room. Educators we have interviewed have all shared how group work has been key to practicing inclusion. While groups are useful, how they are organized is just as important. When you construct groups, students will be looking to find the logic to your grouping—if you group by ability, students will use their grouping to evaluate their position within the ability hierarchy that you have created. For the majority of group work conducted in classrooms, groups should be clearly made at random. Purposively organized groups can also be designed to support class dynamics by assigning roles to students or supporting their own designation of roles so that all students are positioned as active contributors (Rapke, 2019, personal communication). Privileging friendships in group work is also important. For activities targeting particular skills, flexible groupings within the class are possible so long as they do not become permanent.

Sharing Instructions

Teaching requires sharing a lot of instructions. Over the course of a day, educators may instruct students on everything from behavior, transitions, classroom activities, and take-home assignments. For a variety of reasons, many students may have a difficult time retaining multistep directions and often need support either in remembering the sequence of instructions or their application. To improve access, it is important to ensure activity instructions are provided verbally, auditorily, visually (e.g., on the wall/board), and (if possible) accessible through an online platform, particularly if students will be expected to complete from home. Should students have access to technology, such as a phone or device, they can be encouraged to take a photo of the instructions or dictate using speech-to-text software to ensure they can independently access instructions when needed.

Accessible Material

Accessible material is another important consideration when designing inclusive programming. When using different materials in the classroom or asking students to access material at home, we must always be questioning the extent of accessibility with each proposed task. Across jurisdictions, there may be established guidelines that can provide educators with strategies to ensure their material is accessible. For example, in Ontario there is the AODA—Accessibility for Ontarians with Disabilities Act (2005)—which offers guidelines for how to produce accessible texts, websites, and communications. Drawing on the AODA, some quick considerations follow:

Texts

Assigned texts should be available in both print and digital forms. Large-print options and text-to-speech software should also be made available. Recognizing constraints around resources, ideally, students should be able to select the format of their choice as opposed to being singled out and ascribed a format. For example, the use of devices to access digital formats should be made available to all students as opposed to only those who have documented accommodations. Other textual forms include braille and audio formats.

Presentations

The use of slides with a darker background and lighter font can help with visual acuity. Images should include Alt Text Captioning or added captions. If adding voice-over to a presentation, it is also important to provide a transcript that can be read by text-to-speech software.

Media

If showing videos or films in class, closed captioning should be made available and set up before viewing to ensure students do not need to request. If using online platforms for meetings or classes, many offer live close captioning and transcription features.

Communication

The AODA recommends that information be offered through multiple forms, including textual, auditory, and visual formats. When possible, integrating the use of images/picture symbols is also effective for both conceptual learning and instructions. There are a number of established augmentative communication strategies and, with new technological advances, more are being developed all the time. For example, text-to-speech and speech-to-text programs are now available on many phones, tablet devices, and computers. Sign language interpretation may be another resource available to your students. If you are working with Deaf students and have sign language interpreters present in class, as with all students regarding accommodations, it is important to work with the student as to how best they would like to use interpretation within the classroom. Interpretation is a critical tool for Deaf students. To ensure the class understands how interpretation works, it would be helpful to establish class-wide communication strategies to facilitate discussion.

Assessment

Adopting the principles of UDL and differentiated instruction are critically important to assessment. If I am designing an assessment to understand how much students learned throughout a particular curricular unit or on a particular concept, I need to decide through which forms students should be expected to demonstrate their knowledge. Dependent on what elements are being assessed, students might be expected to demonstrate their knowledge through writing, which could include handwriting or composing on a computer. If neither of these approaches enables the student to best demonstrate what they have learned, perhaps they can use voice-to-text programs or share their knowledge orally with their educator. Maybe they can best represent their learning through art, the contribution of a blog-style or podcast report integrating images or audio clips and music. Depending on what is being examined, the approach to assessment should embed flexibility and should not create barriers to students' demonstration of learning. However, it is also critically important that high expectations are maintained and students are not excluded from learning key skills. Mastering skills will serve students both now and in the future. It is important that differentiation maintains the integrity of what is being learned and does not, itself, become a barrier. Throughout this book, we have explored how assessment and notions of ability can be shaped by biases we may hold related to students' identities, histories, and experiences. Therefore, it is important to continuously reflect on our own conclusions as to students' demonstration of ability and/or achievement.

Selecting Disability Positive Texts

Culturally relevant and responsive pedagogy (CRRP) asks educators to ensure that the material selected for their classrooms (e.g., display on the walls, integrate into the curriculum, reading material, themes for discussion) reflect the identities of students within the school and community. In discussions of CRRP, disability culture is rarely included as a critical component to creating equitable classrooms. A challenge for educators is to think about how to integrate the histories and stories of disabled people that challenge charity or medical notions of disability, and instead accurately and positively reflect the contributions of disabled people.

Questions for Further Thought and Reflection

1. In your own practice, which forms of differentiation are you already implementing, and which might you be able to integrate in future?
2. Technology is a significant asset. How does your school acquire access to technology for students? What are some ways to strategically integrate technology into your classroom without stigmatizing students who may depend on it?
3. When you encounter a text that includes disabled characters, what aspects of the text will you consider before integrating it into your course material?

Conclusion: Moving Forward and Setting New Conditions for Justice

"We cannot fight for liberation without a deep, clear understanding of disability, ableism and disability justice."

—MINGUS, 2011, PARA. 18

We began this book with a discussion on rights and justice in schools and will end with ideas of how we might be able to shift the field even further toward disability justice–oriented schooling experiences.

Complicating the Role Rights Have Played in the Schooling of Disabled Children

Access to education through special education emerged from a long struggle for disabled students to have equitable access to public school. Both Canada and the United States shared similar trajectories in terms of mainstreaming disabled students at around the same time. Ellis (2019) summarizes,

> In 1975, the United States Congress passed the Education for All Hand-icapped Children Act (PL 94-142), effectively making mainstreaming legal compulsory. Ontario passed similar legislation in 1980. Bill 82 mandated public education for virtually all school-age youngsters in the

province and integrated some existing separate programs for mentally retarded children into mainstream school buildings. But it stopped short of PL 94-142's "least restrictive environment" language. It did not require boards to include exceptional students in regular graded classrooms. A requirement for integrated placements in regular classrooms would not appear in Ontario schools until further legislative changes forced the issue in the early 1990s. (pp. 208–209)

Along with access to education in Ontario, Bill 82, also known as the Education Amendment Act, 1980, the Ministry of Education established an identification and placement process, arguing that such a process was necessary to ensure identification of need and expeditious placement of disabled students in remedial programs (Stephensen 1978; Reid et al., 2020). The Ontario Ministry of Education states that, "The board's special education plan must be designed to comply with the Canadian Charter of Rights and Freedoms, the Ontario Human Rights Code, the Education Act and regulations made under the act, and any other relevant legislation" (Ontario Ministry of Education, 2017, p. B4). Further, they add that all children "have the right to attend school" (p. C5), that "parents have the right to request that the principal refer their child to an IPRC" (p. D3), and that parents, should they not agree with the IPRC's decision, "have the right to appeal to the Ontario Special Education Tribunal" (p. D32).

Similar reforms have taken place within the United States. In 1990, the Education for All Handicapped Children Act soon evolved into the Individuals with Disabilities Education Act (IDEA) (Brandman University, 2020). IDEA includes students' rights to Free Appropriate Public Education as well as protects parents' rights to request educational assessments, and the right to appeal decisions related to special education. These protections are all granted through federal law. In both jurisdictions, disabled students have the right to access special education, which can include special education supports, provisions, and programming (Ontario Human Rights Commission, 2018, sect. 2.2.1; United States Department of Education, 2017).

Systemic ableism and ongoing barriers facing disabled students in school continues to motivate families to request special education. When general education is not working, many families believe special education offers stop-gap measures to address both structural and pedagogical inequities. The right or entitlement to special education services and programming, integrated into education law or policy, was a win for families. A right to special education not only acknowledged the systemic failure to account for the unique needs of disabled students, but gave families power to advocate for their children within the school system. Yet, rarely are special education outcomes or long-term implications to future education shared with families or educators. So what happens when research reveals that special education can, itself, be a barrier to disabled students?

Responding to Research

Over the past several decades, empirical evidence has shown academic and social benefits of dismantling many special education structures and promoting inclusion (Hehir et al., 2016). Similarly, research has also shown that detracking at the secondary level addresses issues of equity and access in public education (Organisation for Economic Co-operation and Development (OECD), 2012; Lavrijsen & Nicaise, 2015; Matthewes, 2018; Rubin, 2006). Additionally, research continues to show the dangers of ability-grouping and structuring tiered streams for learning (Archer et al., 2018). Program placement (e.g., specialized or special education programming, academic streaming) can play a significant role in students' trajectories and, in terms of long-term outcomes, can often trump student achievement (Parekh & Brown, 2019). Students who have experienced historical marginalization related to racialization, anti-Black or anti-Indigenous discrimination, as well as students in lower income communities are continuously overrepresented in programs and pathways that have restrictive access to postsecondary education (Brown et al., 2021). Students with a history in special education and/or lower academic streaming face limited in post–high school opportunities. Special education may be positioned as a system through which families and disabled students can enact their rights to education, but it has not brought about disability justice in schools.

As education districts attempt to respond to the growing system and international research and work to establish more inclusive policies and practices, they often face notable resistance from families. Resistance can be triggered as a response to a shift in system ideology that no longer aligns with what has been historically accepted as "good practice" and "the way things are done." Resistance can also be triggered by a perceived shift or potential loss of support. For instance, say a child was identified in early elementary and, upon a district's recommendation, subsequently placed in a part-time special education program. Years later, after much convincing that a special education model is the most effective strategy to support this child's learning, the district begins collapsing that very special education program citing that it has been deemed ineffective or even detrimental to students' learning and future prospects. It should not be a surprise when families respond with suspicion, distrust, or hurt. Suspicion, because inclusion does not match their earlier understanding of care and support; distrust that an ulterior motive, like cost-savings, may be at play; and hurt that, should this be true, they may have inadvertently participated in a practice that may have contributed to the further marginalization of their child. This shift toward inclusion, for many families, can feel like a betrayal.

Additionally, while districts grapple with inclusion, many begin with the visible, physical representations of inclusion such as space and placement. Space and placement do count in terms of inclusion, but they are only a piece of the puzzle. Families know that attitudinal barriers, expressed by both students and educators, can also play a significant role in how their child's social, emotional, and academic needs are addressed in the classroom, the school, and on the playground. Therefore, suggesting that their children leave a designated space for disabled learners, and enter a previously determined "inappropriate" general education program, without the necessary anti-ableist work in place, is a scary and often undesirable transition. After generations of being told of the hostile conditions in general education and that the safest and most effective learning environment for their children is special education, inclusion can be a tough sell . . . and rightfully so.

Public education districts require public buy-in and, part of keeping more affluent communities engaged in public education, is achieved by offering parents' choice in the kinds of programs their children can access. Families with more privilege are often a driving force in discussions of school choice and the push for schools to offer enriched programming such as advanced placement, specialty arts, or International Baccalaureate programs. In discussions around streaming, school district representatives often brought up the issue that if elite programs were not offered, affluent families would abandon public education for the private system. This is similar for special education. If more families believe that their children are not being served within the public education system, there is real concern that families with economic means will leave the district entirely to seek out private specialized education alternatives. With resistance to inclusion among families and the risk of decreasing enrollment, many districts become dissuaded from promoting inclusion or restructuring their special education practices (Parekh, 2020).

Keenly aware of this tension, the United Nation's Committee on the Rights of Persons with Disabilities felt it important to clarify its position on inclusive programming and parental choice. In a General Comment (no. 4), point 4, the committee begins by pointing to the importance of data and research for the purposes of system accountability to inform inclusive programming, policy, and interventions. The committee then articulates, in point 10, that,

> *"Inclusive education is to be understood as:*
> *A fundamental human right of all learners. Notably, education is the right of the individual learner, and not, in the case of children, the right of a parent or caregiver. Parental responsibilities in this regard are subordinate to the rights of the child."* (United Nations, 2016, p. 3)

This is a powerful and, to many families, controversial statement. As stated, regardless of parent desire to place their children in programs with which they are more comfortable, the obligation on behalf of schools and school districts is to uphold the rights of the learner. As research generally supports inclusion and the elimination of exclusionary practices, would districts not then be obligated to ensure students have access to inclusive learning environments? This puts school districts in a unique position, one that can be in direct conflict with the very population they are dependent on. What is particularly powerful about this statement from the Committee on the Rights of Persons with Disabilities is that it directly centers the experience of disabled children. This centering of disabled experiences in school edges us toward greater realization of disability justice in education.

As we have discussed throughout this book, special education is tethered to a deficit ideology that can produce harm in both its function and outcomes for students. So we have to ask ourselves, "Who benefits from special education?" (Brantlinger, 2006). As the title queries, Brantlinger (2006) aptly pointed out that while many students may not necessarily benefit directly from special education or the process of identification, there are a number of groups that do: test producers, politicians, political pundits, advocates for the privatization of education, school superintendents, professionals and education-related professions. As Brantlinger (2006) notes, "expanding numbers of specialists and technical experts correspond to burgeoning numbers of abnormalities and pathologies" (p. 216). Lastly, but not the least benefited, Brantlinger (2006) cites the educated middle class.

Special education positions disability as located within the individual and as something to be fixed through identification processes, accommodations and specialized placements, often delivered outside the general classroom (Brantlinger, 2006). Even though special education is a historically established system in Canadian and American public schools, it rarely accounts for or is required to demonstrate its effectiveness in promoting students' academic achievement. In fact, research suggests that deficit-oriented programming does not work, and the ways in which students are organized into special education programs creates a significant problem, particularly for racial minority and students living in poverty (Mitchell, 2015). As noted, compared to special education placements, studies show that students' academic learning in inclusive placements tend to show either no difference or significantly improved achievement (Parekh, 2013). In contrast, when studied, special education is rarely (if ever) identified as the more effective approach (Baker, 2002; Mitchell 2010/2015).

Modeling Inclusion

How students are organized matters. Who decides *who* and *how* to include sends important messages around *who* and *what* we value as a society. As a new researcher, I was once invited to visit another school district that held, at the time, a radically different view on special education and inclusion. Our district had close to three times the proportion of self-contained special education programs compared to those outside the urban core (Brown, et al., 2016). In contrast, their large district had a handful of special education programs which, from what I was told, were strictly time limited. During my visit, I toured schools and observed classrooms, both elementary and secondary, in which disabled students were fully included and supported within the general classroom. It was clear that many supports had been intentionally integrated into the classroom program to promote inclusion.

Following the tour, the district leader shared that most of the educators hired to the system had also grown up in the district and arrived to their work ready to practice the principles of inclusion they had learned and experienced as youth. Since so much of our understanding around learning is shaped by the conditions in which we were schooled, this made a lot of sense. Many educators and administrators shared the system's commitment to inclusion and adopted the view that practicing inclusion in school set youth up to embrace and create a more inclusive society. Their commitment to inclusion, in part, was to be sure that students could go through life understanding and appreciating human difference. In their opinion, inclusion removed a great deal of anxiety and suspicion around disability and that stigma was further stoked by segregated or self-contained practices. Disability can arrive to anyone, at any time, and they wanted their youth to be comfortable in relationship with disabled peers, siblings, parents, and grandparents. They did not see inclusion as a school-specific issue, but rather, holistically, as a vision for society that promoted care and interdependent relationships. Through its notable commitment to disability inclusion and normalization of disability as part of the human experience, this district was producing citizens who shared a different understanding of disability, one they integrated into their work and communities.

Inclusion's Important . . . but What About Justice?

As mentioned earlier, as a result of extensive research and advocacy, the right to inclusive education is enshrined in the Convention on the Rights of Persons with Disabilities (Article 24) (United Nations, 2006) and is often described as "the right approach" for educating disabled children. Yet debate around what inclusion really means and how we can implement it within the current structure of public schooling is ongoing (De Beco, 2017). So, if inclusion is the right approach to education, are we approaching inclusion in the right way? Is the very act of being together and supported together enough to meet the aims of disability justice? I would argue that it could be a good start but I would also argue that it does not go far enough.

Despite all the research, advocacy, and activism around disability rights and education, in many school systems across North America, we continue making decisions based upon inconsistent and outdated conceptualizations of inclusion. Typical notions of inclusion detail the provision of special education supports—but doing so in the general classroom as opposed to a special education program. To promote justice, we must do more than ensure access to classrooms, curriculum, and supports. If our intention is to achieve disability justice in schools, we need a cultural shift in how we think about schooling: one that acknowledges disability identity, incorporates disability culture, teaches disability history, and challenges all forms of ableism.

When it comes to disability in schools, we appear to have an unrelenting preoccupation with three determinations: What is "wrong" with students, where should they be taught, and what can we give them to successfully "fit in" to general education? In discourses on inclusion, too often we omit broader, more-complex notions of disability identity. We rarely discuss how disability identity can be included and reflected within the school curriculum and honored within classroom practices. Equity discussions involving disability seem to stall at whether students have access to accommodations and modifications. Accommodations may allow students to be successful in engaging with their academic studies, but accommodations, alone, do not produce inclusion—let alone justice.

Ableism in schools perpetuates the notion that disability is somehow inferior, something that elicits shame. Exacerbating the ability divide, schools are rife with competition and flawed notions of meritocracy. In schools, high achievement and perceived potential are rewarded with status and privilege. But as Brantlinger (2006) notes, to have "winners," we also have to have "losers" (p. 197). For all the students whose ability we champion and celebrate, there are students who have been equally judged as "lacking." As a result of systemic discrimination, schools do not see disability or disabled identities as political or as having power. The activities disabled students perform and the spaces they occupy are often devalued. Other historically marginalized groups have faced similar discriminatory attitudes and flawed assumptions around their capacity, their culture, and their identity, and have asserted their collective power to effect change in education. Part of their advocacy includes claiming space in schools, through curriculum and community, to ensure students can engage in intentional instruction, community building, and political organization. As activism often builds on the work forged by earlier movements, perhaps these initiatives could inspire innovative approaches to disability justice in schools.

Truth and Reconciliation

Canada and the United States have a long history of systemic racism, oppression, and genocide of Indigenous peoples (Branscome, 2013; MacDonald & Hudson, 2012; Whyte, 2016). In the 19th and 20th centuries, both nations supported a residential school system for Indigenous youth resulting in horrific outcomes for Indigenous communities (Regan, 2010; Woolford, 2015). In residential schools, Indigenous children were not allowed to engage in their cultural activities or languages. They were forced to adopt unfamiliar cultural practices and, while the institutions were labeled as schools, they offered substandard education. Instead of learning, many children within the residential school system were largely required to perform manual labor (Toulouse, 2018).

The residential school system for Indigenous youth is one of the United States and Canada's most shameful practices. In their book,

Disability Incarcerated: Imprisonment and Disability in the United States and Canada, authors draw on the parallels between the historical treatment of Indigenous youth and disabled children, particularly in their eugenic ideology (Ben-Moshe et al., 2014). Although many differences exist, residential schools for Indigenous children and the institutionalization of disabled youth share similarities in their history, structure, and purpose. For example, both systems were established on the assumption that families and communities were unreliable and incapable of raising and supporting their own children. Both were sites where children died from abuse and neglect (Appleman, 2018; Kassam, 2018). In fact, just recently in Canada (2021), over 1000 bodies of Indigenous children, thus far, have been located following their deaths and burials at residential schools (Weisberger, 2021). This staggering figure is hauntingly similar to the number of unmarked graves located on the grounds of Ontario's Huronia Regional Centre, Canada's oldest institution for disabled people (Alamenciak, 2014). Both systems were founded on the principles of assimilation, believing that indoctrination in a Eurocentric, colonialist, and ableist worldview would benefit society. Both systems were believed to occupy essential roles in maintaining cultural (white supremacist and ableist) norms and values in society

In 2015, The Truth and Reconciliation Commission of Canada (TRC) released their *Calls to Action* report which included a number of action items related to the education system (Truth & Reconciliation Commission, 2015a). Within these calls to action, the commission asked the Canadian government to commit, in partnership with Indigenous people, to close educational gaps for Indigenous people as well as fund the development of culturally appropriate curricula (Truth & Reconciliation Commission, 2015a). The document recognizes the key importance of all levels of education including early childhood education programs to postsecondary education access. While there has not yet been a formal national recognition or reconciliation of the institutional system for disabled people, there have been formal apologies issued and settlements reached over neglect and abuse experienced within institutions (Rossiter & Rinaldi, 2018).

Drawing on the TRC's *Calls to Action,* access to education as well as Indigenous centered and Indigenous informed pedagogy are critically important to emancipation. I believe similar recommendations related to disability and education would also be effective. A commitment to access across all education sectors—including the development of curricula—in partnership with disabled persons and disabled persons organizations, would be a positive move forward in promoting disability justice in schools.

Africentric* Schooling

Black students have long experienced barriers and trauma in public education schools (James, 1995; Gillborn, 2018) and many Black families have sought an alternative option (Shapiro, 2019). In both Canada and the United States, there has been a long history of segregated schooling for Black students. In 1954, the Supreme Court case *Brown v. Board of Education* marked a formal end to racial segregation in American schools (Library of Congress, n.d.), although informal segregation continues. As education is provincially mandated in Canada, it was up to each province to outlaw racial segregation in schools. The last racially segregated school in Ontario closed in 1965 whereas Nova Scotia did not officially close their remaining segregated school until 1983 (Henry, 2019).

Part of the rationalization of racially integrated schools was to strategically share resources that support student learning. However, despite intentions, structural racism persists, leaving, in particular, Black and Indigenous students at a significant disadvantage. To counter the white, Eurocentricity of public schooling, Africentric education shapes the curriculum and guides material selection. A study examining the impact of Africentric curriculum on Black student achievement also identified the criteria used by US curriculum writers to determine which elements to include in an Africentric history curriculum (Duncan, 2012):

1. *The scope is not solely African but seeks to undermine a racist hegemony that benefits Whites to the detriment of those determined as Other.*

---

* In Canada, "Afrocentric" schooling is referred to as "Africentric" schooling.

2. *The curriculum supports and includes epistemological positions that are divergent from the normative.*
3. *Valid knowledge is not limited to what can be "linguistically articulated" (Abdi, 2006, p. 17) due to the belief that an over reliance on sensory perception restricts knowledge.*
4. *The curriculum is composed of body, mind, and spirit so that the objective and subjective coexist without contradiction (Duncan, 2012, pp. 92–93).*

Africentric schooling commits to three key outcomes—high achievement, self-pride, and motivation (Toronto District School Board, 2020). To achieve these outcomes, Africentric education centers the histories, knowledge, and experiences of people of African descent and commits to the inclusion of diverse perspectives within the curriculum. Students engaging in Africentric education learn about Black pride, culture, and identity, how to identify and address racism and racial inequality, as well as are exposed to curricula relevant to the Black student experience.

When I consider the approach to Africentric education, I think about the potential for how a similar curricular framework could empower disabled students. I see potential in the opportunity for students to engage in curriculum that addresses the politics of disability, how ability and disability are socially constructed, and how to identify and navigate ableism. Imagine a curriculum designed by disabled people and taught by disabled educators, that sought to undermine ableist ideologies, included divergent perspectives, and embraced disabled knowledges.

Gay–Straight Alliances

The final example of identity-based groups establishing new forms of organization and in-school learning are gay–straight alliances (GSAs). GSAs are often organized as high school clubs that promote awareness of issues affecting the Lesbian, Gay, Bisexual, Transgender, Queer, Two-Spirit +(LGBTQ2S+) community. GSAs promote acceptance of diverse genders and sexualities. Through their advocacy work, GSAs attempt to address in-school homophobia and create safer spaces for LGBTQ2S+ youth (Callaghan, 2014).

GSAs in high schools were established in Massachusetts in 1988 (Storer, 2008). LGBTQ2S+ youth have long experienced, and reported, experiences of harassment and bullying in school (Centre for Sexuality, 2020). My own research has shown that youth who identify as LGBTQ2S+ experience significant exclusion in school coupled with concerns around safety (Parekh, 2014). A key feature of high school GSAs is that they are supported by educators, but are ultimately youth led. As identified by the Centre for Sexuality, GSAs "provide a safe space for students to meet, socialize and support one another as they discuss their feelings and experiences related to sexual orientation and gender identity. Clubs often work on advocacy, human rights and awareness projects to make their schools and communities better places to live for all" (Centre for Sexuality, 2020, para. 2). As authors Stonefish and Lafreniere (2015) write, GSAs not only provide greater learning and education for students but they also provide opportunities for social activism in relation to gender and sexuality discrimination. GSAs have not been without their controversy. Since their inception, GSAs have faced pressures, exclusions, and bans, particularly in Catholic education systems and in conservative-led areas (Callaghan, 2014; Colletta, 2019). However, GSAs can play a critical role in engaging youth in exercising their rights, identifying, and navigating homophobia, transphobia, and gender discrimination.

What Could This Mean for Disability and Education?

These three examples of curricular and student-led initiatives demonstrate how education can be a key site for reparation and promotion of antidiscrimination. Paramount to each is what students are learning, whom they are learning with and from, and what opportunities exist for youth-led engagement and activism as related to their own experiences. The TRC's *Calls to Action* report (Truth & Reconciliation Commission, 2015a) makes it clear that access alone is insufficient. In partnership with people who share an identity and culture, the development of curriculum is also important. It is not enough to provide an inclusive curriculum or space to connect—drawing on the tenets of disability justice (Berne, 2015), these curricula and spaces need to be led by those most marginalized by ableism within the education system. These commitments emphasize the critical place education holds in supporting students' academic trajectories, shaping students' worldviews, and arming students with the necessary skills to challenge the systems that disable them.

The TRC's Justice Murray Sinclair echoes this optimism by stating "[e]ducation is what got us into this mess—the use of education at least in terms of residential schools—but education is the key to reconciliation" (Sinclair, as cited in Watters, 2015, para. 17). According to Madden (2019), Sinclair's sentiment was reinforced in the summary section of the final TRC report (Truth and Reconciliation Commission of Canada, 2015b) arguing that education has led to "intergenerational trauma" and that what is and is not taught in schools has lasting impacts on us all (Madden, 2019).

When schools and curriculum are designed to address and support students' identities and experiences, there are opportunities to nurture a sense of belonging, community building, and to prepare students with the critical framework and navigational skills they will need to address systemic discrimination. Likewise, the establishments of GSAs in high schools provide opportunities for important education on identity and experience. These opportunities also enable students to lead and engage in politics and social activism. From these examples, we can draw a great deal of insight on how we can better support disabled youth in schools.

As part of our work as educators, we need to recognize that we, ourselves, have been schooled in an ableist system and taught to teach with ableist principles. Throughout our own education, in our classrooms and schools, we have been grouped by our ability, as well as have been offered or denied opportunities in relation to how others have perceived our ability. We have arrived to the field of education as educators, in many ways, due to the decisions others have made on our behalf—to pass us, promote us, recommend us. And throughout, many of us were unaware of how we were being organized in school—or we understood our organization to be a result of neutral decisions. As educators, we work in ableist systems that produce and reproduce inequity justified by students' perceived ability, perceptions constructed by systemic discrimination. How do we address and interrupt our reproduction of ableism in the classes we teach? How do we assess and evaluate without bias? How do we center the experiences of disabled students and integrate disability culture within our classrooms?

We need to, first, recognize that the work is ongoing. Interrupting ableism requires us to approach all aspects of pedagogy and curriculum, assessment and evaluation, our language, who and what we privilege in our classrooms, and how we address perceived differences in ability within our students. We have to normalize difference, make sure our classrooms are safe to express difference, and respond to difference. We need to listen and learn from those who have been asked to navigate ableist structures, have experienced exclusion; we must be guided by their experience, insights, and expertise. In discussions around inclusion, one administrator shared that inclusion is not something we can "do to" students, it has to be something we cocreate in partnership with students. When it comes to designing and identifying what needs to be integrated into the classroom, into our practice, into our teaching to effectively address ableism, we must center disabled students' insights and experiences. But disability justice can only be achieved in solidarity with other justice-seeking movements, particularly those organizing around racial, class, and sexual identity discrimination. Disability justice requires an understanding that constructions of disability and madness can be influenced by racial, class, sexual, and gender identity discrimination. Therefore, students who face multiple sites of oppression in school are often in the best position to identify the implicit and explicit exclusions hidden within curriculum and pedagogical practice.

Disability Futures in Schools

Enabling disabled youth to engage in positive identity construction, the disruption of ableism and exclusion, and centering disabled knowledges could ignite a radical movement within education. De Beco writes, "If the right to inclusive education can be understood in a manner that fully takes into account its application, the general education system would be one in which the participation of disabled children would be incorporated into its very own values" (2017, p. 16). Imagine a curriculum created and guided by disabled people and disabled people's organizations. Imagine classroom practices that are designed to nurture and promote disability identity, disability community, as well as to teach students how to identify and address ableism. Imagine spaces for disabled youth where they can connect and organize for the purpose of political and social activism. Imagine schooling in which the notion of "disability as deficit" is replaced with "disability pride."

Ideas like this are catching on and it is an exciting time to be in education. Critical work is being done on anti-ableist activism, disability solidarity, and the role schools can play. Access to accommodations, modifications, and integrated placements are insufficient to the task of promoting disability justice. Offering students learning tools and expecting them to work through an ableist curriculum and toxic classroom climate is simply not enough. Being denied the opportunity to engage in activism and the purposeful disruption of disability oppression is no longer acceptable. We need to do better for our students. What happens in schools matters. In schools, how bodies are organized matters, who organizes bodies matters, and how value is ascribed to bodies matters. At every level of education, we need disabled students, educators, and leaders guiding how we organize, support, and celebrate students. Sins Invalid (n.d.), a disability justice based performance organization, states as part of their mission that

> *Sins Invalid recognizes that we will be liberated as whole beings—as disabled, as queer, as brown, as black, as gender non-conforming, as trans, as women, as men, as non-binary gendered—we are far greater whole than partitioned. We recognize that our allies emerge from many communities and that demographic identity alone does not determine one's commitment to liberation.* (n.d., para. 3)

This statement invites all of us, with all parts of our being, to engage in the work of disability justice, as it is key to the emancipation to justice-seeking groups. Schools are an excellent site for this work and offer endless possibilities of what can be imagined.

References

Abdi, A. (2006). Eurocentric discourses and African philosophies and epistemologies of education: Counter-hegemonic analyses and responses. *International Education, 36*(1), 15–31. Retrieved from http://search.ebscohost.com.ezproxy.apollolibrary.com

Accessibility for Ontarians with Disabilities Act (AODA) (2005). https://www.ontario.ca/laws/statute/05a11

Alamenciak, T. (2014). Remembering the dead at Huronia Regional Centre. Toronto Star. (Dec. 29, 2014). https://www.thestar.com/news/gta/2014/12/29/remembering_the_dead_at_huronia_regional_centre.html

Annamma, S., & Morrison, D. (2018). Identifying dysfunctional education ecologies: A DisCrit analysis of bias in the classroom. Equity & Excellence in Education, 51(2), 114–131. https://doi.org/10.1080/10665684.2018.1496047

Appleman, L. (2018). Deviancy, dependency, and disability: The forgotten history of eugenics and mass incarceration. *Duke Law Journal, 68*(3), 417–478.

Archer, L., Francis, B., Miller, S., Taylor, B., Tereshchenko, A., Mazenod, A., Pepper, D., & Travers, M.-C. (2018). The symbolic violence of setting: A Bourdieusian analysis of mixed methods data on secondary students' views about setting. *British Educational Research Journal, 44*(1), 119–140.

Artiles, A., Kozleski, E., Trent, S., Osher, D., & Ortiz, A. (2010).

Justifying and explaining disproportionality, 1968–2008: A critique of underlying views of culture. *Exceptional Children, 76*(3), 279–299.

Artiles, A. J., Kozleski, E. B., & Waitoller, F. R. (2011). *Inclusive education: Examining equity on five continents*. Harvard Education Press.

Baglieri, S., & Lalvani, P. (2020). *Undoing ableism: Teaching about disability in K–12 classrooms*. Routledge.

Baker, B. (2002). The hunt for disability: The new eugenics and the normalization of school children. *Teachers' College Record, 104*(4), 663–703.

Barshay, J. (2016). *Bright Black students taught by Black teachers are more likely to get into gifted-and-talented classrooms. The Hechinger Report.* https://hechingerreport.org/bright-black-students-who-are-taught -by-black-teachers-are-more-likely-to-get-into-gifted-and-talented -classrooms/

Ben-Moshe, L., Chapman, C., & Carey, A. (Eds.). *Disability incarcerated: Imprisonment and disability in the United States and Canada*. Palgrave MacMillan.

Berman, D. L., & Connor, D. J. (2017_). *A child, a family, a school, a community: A tale of inclusive education*. Peter Lang.

Berne, P. (2015). Disability justice – a working draft by Patty Berne. https://www.sinsinvalid.org/blog/disability-justice-a-working-draft-by -patty-berne

Bourdieu, P. (1973). Cultural reproduction and social reproduction, in Richard Brown (Ed.) *Knowledge, Education, and Cultural Change* (pp. 71–112). London: Tavistock.

Bowal, P., & Pecson, K. (2011). Eugenics and Leilani Muir. *Lawnow, 35*(5), 49–52.

Braddock, D., & Parish, S. (2001). An institutional history of disability. In: Albrecht, G.L., Seelman, K.D., Bury, M., (Eds). *Handbook of disability studies*. Thousand Oaks: Sage. 11–68.

Brandman University. (2020, January 30). 4 Special education laws and policies every teacher should know. https://www.brandman.edu/ news-and-events/blog/special-education-laws

Branscome, B. (2013). Oppression on Indigenous Peoples. [Technical Report]. DOI:10.13140/2.1.3713.4720

Brantlinger, E. (2006). (Ed) *Who benefits from special education? Remediating (fixing) other people's children*. Lawrence Erlbaum.

Bronfenbrenner, U. (1986). Ecology of the family as a context for human development: Research perspectives. *Developmental Psychology, 22*(6), 723–742.

Bronfenbrenner, U. (1992). Ecological systems theory. In R. Vasta (Ed.), *Six theories of child development: Revised formulations and current issues* (p. 187–249). Jessica Kingsley.

Brown, L. (2016, May 23). TDSB's specialty schools all but forgotten. *The Toronto Star*. https://www.thestar.com/yourtoronto/education/2016/05/23/tdsbs-specialty-schools-all-but-forgotten.html

Brown, R. S., Newton, L., Tam, G., & Parekh, G. (2016). *The trajectories of grade 9 mathematics achievement 2008–2013* (Report No. 15/16-05). Toronto District School Board.

Brown, R. S., & Parekh, G. (2010). *Special education: Structural overview and student demographics* (Report No. 10/11-03). Toronto District School Board.

Brown, R. S., Parekh, G., & Abdulkarim, F. (2021). Special education in the TDSB: A re-examination of system trends, 2006/07–2016/17. Toronto District School Board.

Brown, R. S., Parekh, G., & Gallagher-MacKay, K. (2018). *Getting through secondary school: The example of mathematics in recent TDSB grade 9 cohorts* [Presentation]. Higher Education Quality Council of Ontario, Toronto.

Brown, R. S., Parekh, G., & Marmureanu, C. (2016). *Special Education in the Toronto District School Board: Trends and comparisons to Ontario* (Report No. 1/17–07). Toronto: Toronto District School Board.

Brown, R. S., Parekh, G., & Presley, A. (2013). *The TDSB grade 9 education* (Fact Sheet No. 4). Toronto District School Board.

Brown, R. S., Parekh, G., & Zheng, S. (In progress). *Middle-school decisions and post-secondary access: Exploring the role of modified curriculum in mathematics*.

Bui, S., Imberman, S., & Craig, S. (2012). Poor results for high achievers. *Education Next, 12*(1), 70–76.

Callaghan, T. D. (2014). Law and disorder: Ontario Catholic bishops' opposition to Gay-Straight Alliances. *Paideusis, 22*(1), 28–37.

Castagno, A. (2014). *Education in whiteness: Good intentions and diversity in schools.* University of Minnesota Press.

Center for Parent Information and Resources. (2017). The short and sweet IEP overview. https://www.parentcenterhub.org/iep-overview/

Centre for Sexuality. (2020). Gay-Straight Alliances. https://understandingtheguidelines.ca/faqs/gay-straight-alliances/

Chapman, C., & Withers, A. J. (2019). *A violent history of benevolence: Interlocking oppression in the moral economies of social working.* University of Toronto Press.

Chatoor, K. (2021). *Postsecondary Credential Attainment and Labour Market Outcomes for Ontario Students with Disabilities.* Toronto: Higher Education Quality Council of Ontario.

Colletta, A. (2019, July 6). Alberta's new conservative government revisits gay-straight student alliances. *The Washington Post.* https://www.washingtonpost.com/world/the_americas/albertas-new-conservative-government-revisits-gay-straight-student-alliances/2019/07/05/114fd9ce-98fa-11e9-9a16-dc551ea5a43b_story.html

Connor, D. J. & Annamma, S. (2014). In Lawrence-Brown, D., & Sapon-Shevin, M. (Eds). *Condition critical: Key principles for equitable and inclusive education.* (pp. 133–153). Teachers College Press.

Connor, D. J. (2017). Who is responsible for the racialized practices evident within (special) education and what can be done to change them? *Theory Into Practice, 56*(3), 226–233. https://doi.org/10.1080/00405841.2017.1336034

Connor, D. J. (2019). Why is special education so afraid of disability studies? Analyzing attacks of disdain and distortion from leaders in the field. *Journal of Curriculum Theorizing, 34*(1), 10–23.

Cooper, J. M. (2006). Classroom teaching skills (8th ed.) Wadsworth Publishing: Belmont, CA.

Cosier, M., & Ashby, C. (2016). *Enacting change from within: Disability studies meet teaching and teacher education.* Peter Lang.

Danforth, S., Taff, S., & Ferguson, P. M. (2006). Place, profession, and program in the history of special education curriculum. In Ellen A. Brantlinger (Ed.). *Who benefits from special education? Remediating (fixing) other people's children* (pp. 1–26). Lawrence Erlbaum.

Davis, L. (2013). Introduction: Disability, normality and power. *The disability studies reader* (pp. 1–14). Taylor and Francis.

De Beco, G. (2017). The right to inclusive education: Why is there so much opposition to its implementation? *International Journal of Law in Context, 14*(3), 396–415. https://doi.org/10.1017/S1744552317000532

De Valenzuela, J. S., Copeland, S., Qi, C. H., & Park, M. (2006). Examining educational equity: Revisiting the disproportionate representation of minority students in special education. *Exceptional Children, 72*(4), 425–441.

DenHoed, A. (2016). The forgotten lessons of the American eugenics movement. The New Yorker. https://www.newyorker.com/books/page-turner/the-forgotten-lessons-of-the-american-eugenics-movement

Dineen, T. (1996). *Manufacturing victims: What the psychology industry is doing to people.* Robert Davies.

Dolmage, J. (2017). *Academic ableism: Disability and higher education.* University of Michigan Press.

Domina, T., Penner, A., & Penner, E. (2017). Categorical inequality: Schools as sorting machines. *Annual Review of Sociology, 43*, 311–330.

Duncan, W. (2012). The effects of Africentric United States history curriculum on Black student achievement. *Contemporary Issues In Education Research—Second Quarter, 5*(2), 91–96. https://files.eric.ed.gov/fulltext/EJ1073186.pdf

Duncan-Andrade, J. M. R., & Morrell, E. (2008). *The art of critical pedagogy: Possibilities for moving from theory to practice in urban schools.* Peter Lang.

Dupré, M. (2012). Disability culture and cultural competency in social work. *Social Work Education, 31*(2), 168–183. https://doi.org/10.1080/02615479.2012.644945

Education Quality and Accountability Office. (n.d.). https://www.eqao.com

Ellis, J. (2019). *A class by themselves? The origins of special education in Toronto and beyond.* University of Toronto Press.

Ellwand, G. (n.d.). *Forced sterilization: How the law righted an ugly wrong in Alberta history.* The Canadian Bar Association, Alberta branch. https://www.cba-alberta.org/Publications-Resources/Resources/Law-Matters/

Law-Matters-Summer-2017/Forced-Sterilization-br-How-the-Law -Righted-An-Ugl

Erevelles, N., Kanga, A., & Middleton, R. (2006). How does it feel to be a problem? Race, disability, and exclusion in educational policy. In Ellen A. Brantlinger (Ed.), *Who benefits from special education? Remediating (fixing) other people's children* (pp. 77–100). Lawrence Erlbaum.

European Agency for Development in Special Needs Education (EADSNE). (2001). Inclusive and effective classroom practices (Edited by C. J. W. Meijer). https://www.european-agency.org/sites/default/ files/inclusive-education-and-effective-classroom-practice_IECP -Literature-Review.pdf

European Agency for Development in Special Needs Education (EADSNE). (2004). Inclusive education and classroom practice in secondary education: Literature review (Edited by C. J. W. Meijer). https://www.european-agency.org/sites/default/ files/inclusive-education-and-effective-classroom-practice_IECP -secondary-Literature-Review.pdf

Fagen, E. (2013). Leilani Muir: Eugenics on trial in Canada. *Peace and Conflict: Journal of Peace Psychology, 19*(4), 358–361. https://doi.org/10 .1037/a0034603

Farley, L. (2018). *Childhood beyond pathology: A psychoanalytic study of development and diagnosis.* State University of New York Press.

Feldman, H. M., & Sutcliffe, T. L. (2009). Chapter 1: The history of developmental-behavioral pediatrics. In W. Carey, A. Crocker, E. Roy Elias, H. Feldman, & W. Coleman (Eds.), *Developmental-behavioral pediatrics* (4th ed., pp. 1–12*).* Saunders.

Ferri, B. (2016). Reimagining response to intervention (RTI). In M. Cosier and C. Ashby (Eds). *Enacting change from within: Disability studies meets teaching and teacher education.* Peter Lang. 153–165.

Ferri, B. A., & Connor, D. J. (2005). Tools of exclusion: Race, disability, and (re)segregated education. *Teachers College Record, 107*(3), 453–474.

Fonseca, R., & Zheng, Y. (2011). The effect of education on health: Cross-country evidence. Working Paper. Rand Labor and Population.

Ford, B. (2014). *Diagnosing eligibility for college accommodations: MID, BIF, LD and the* DSM-5. Education Connections. http://educationalconnections

.ca/articles/101%20Diagnosing%20Eligibility%20for%20College%20Accommodations2.pdf

Freire, P. (2000). *Pedagogy of the oppressed*. Bloomsbury Academic; 3rd edition

Gabel, S. (2005). *Disability studies in education: Readings in theory and method*. Peter Lang.

Galton, F. (1869). *Hereditary genius: An inquiry into its laws and consequences*. Macmillan.

Gay, G. (2015). The what, why, and how of culturally responsive teaching: International mandates, challenges, and opportunities. *Multicultural Education Review, 7*(3), 123–139. https://doi.org/10.1080/2005615X.2015.1072079

Gaztambide-Fernández, R. (2013). Why the arts don't *do* anything: Toward a new vision for cultural production in education. *Harvard Educational Review, 83*(1), 211.

Gaztambide-Fernández, R., & Parekh, G. (2017). Market "choices" or structured pathways? How specialized arts education contributes to the reproduction of inequality. *Educational Policy Analysis and Archives, 25*(41), 1–31

Gaztambide-Fernández, R., Saifer, A., & Desai, C. (2013). "Talent" and the misrecognition of social advantage in specialized arts education. *Roeper Review, 35*(2), 124–135.

Giangreco, M. F. (1996). "The stairs didn't go anywhere!" A self-advocate's reflections on specialized services and their impact on people with disabilities [Invited interview]. *Physical Disabilities: Education and Related Services, 14*(2), 1–12.

Gibbons, A. & Warne, R. (2019). First publication of subtests in the Standford-Binet 5, WAIS-IV, WISC-V, and WPPSI-IV. Intelligence, 75, 9-18.

Gillborn, D. (2018). Heads I win, tails you lose: Anti-Black racism as fluid, relentless, individual and systemic. *Peabody Journal of Education, 93*(1), 66–77. https://doi.org/10.1080/0161956X.2017.1403178

Gladwell, M. (2006, May 25-28). *Behavior in the blink of an eye* [Conference presentation]. Association for Psychological Science, 18th Annual Convention, New York, NY, United States. Retrieved from https://vimeo.com/39436914

Gleeson, B. J. (1997). Disability studies: A historical materialist view. *Disability & Society, 12*(2), 179–202.

Gleeson, B. J. (1999). *Geographies of disability.* Routledge.

Goodley, D. (2014). *Dis/ability studies: Theorising disablism and ableism.* Routledge.

Gould, S. J. (1984). Carrie Buck's daughter. Constitutional commentary. Vol. 2, 331–339. https://conservancy.umn.edu/bitstream/handle/11299/164572/02_02_Gould.pdf

Gould, S. J. (1996). *The mismeasure of man.* W. W. Norton.

Greenstein, A. (2016). *Radical inclusive education: Disability, teaching and struggles for liberation.* Routledge.

Habib, D. (2014). *Disabling segregation* [Video]. TED Conferences. https://www.youtube.com/watch?v=izkN5vLbnw8

Hall, M. C., (2019). Critical disability theory. In Edward N. Zalta (Ed.), *The Stanford encyclopedia of philosophy* (Winter 2019 Ed.). https://plato.stanford.edu/archives/win2019/entries/disability-critical

Halseth, R., & Greenwood, M. (2019). *Indigenous early childhood development in Canada: Current state of knowledge and future directions.* National Collaborating Centre for Aboriginal Health.

Hatt, B. (2012). Smartness as a cultural practice in schools. *American Educational Research Journal, 49*(3), 438–460.

Hattie, J. (2009). *Visible learning: A synthesis of over 800 meta-analyses relating to achievement.* Routledge.

Hayden, A. (2020, September 15). *Ableism and white supremacy are intertwined—We must confront them together.* Truthout. https://truthout.org/articles/ableism-and-white-supremacy-are-intertwined-we-must-confront-them-together/

Hehir, T., Grindal, T., Freeman, B., Lamoreau, R., Borquaye, Y., & Burke, S. (2016). *A summary of the evidence on inclusive education.* Instituto Alana & Abt Assoc.

Henry, N. (2019). Racial segregation of Black people in Canada. *The Canadian encyclopedia.* https://www.thecanadianencyclopedia.ca/en/article/racial-segregation-of-black-people-in-canada

Howard, T., Dresser, S. G., & Dunklee, D. R. (2009). Poverty is not a learning disability: Equalizing opportunities for low SES students. Corwin Press.

Houtveen, T., & Van de Grift, W. (2001). Inclusion and adaptive instruction in elementary education. *Journal of Education for Students Placed at Risk, 6*(4), 389–409.

Ineese-Nash, N., Bomberry, Y., Underwood, K., & Hache, A. (2017). Raising a child within early childhood dis-ability support systems Shakonehya: ra's ne shakoyen'okon:'a G'chi-gshkewesiwad binoonhyag ᏏᎾᏛᎦ ᏈᏟᎡᎠ ᎠᎠᎤᏅᎤ ᏏᎾᏛᎦ ᏃᎠᎤᏈᏋᏃ: Ga-Miinigoowozid Gikendaagoosowin Awaazigish, Ga-Miinigoowozid Ga-Izhichigetan. Indigenous Policy Journal, *28*(3).

Ireton, J. (2021 March). *Canada's nursing homes have worst record for COVID-19 deaths among wealthy nations: Report.* Canadian Broadcasting Corporation. https://www.cbc.ca/news/canada/ottawa/canada-record-covid-19-deaths-wealthy-countries-cihi-1.5968749

Irwin, N. (2015, April 15). Paltry pay: Why American workers without much education are being hammered. *The New York Times*, A3.

James, C. E., (1995). Multicultural and anti-racism education in Canada. *Race, Gender & Class, 2*(3)*,* 31–48

James, A., & James, A. (2012). Developmentalism. In *Key concepts in childhood studies* (pp. 42–44). SAGE. https://doi.org/10.4135/9781526435613.n19

Kassam, A. (2018). Canada sued over years of alleged experimentation on Indigenous people. *The Guardian.* https://www.theguardian.com/world/2018/may/11/canada-indigenous-people-medical-experiments-lawsuit

Kearney, M., Hershbein, B., & Jacome, E. (2015). *Profiles of change: Employment, earnings and occupations from 1990–2013.* Brookings Institute.

Kendi, I. X. (2019). *How to be an antiracist.* One World.

Ladson-Billings, G. (1995). But that's just good teaching! The case for culturally relevant pedagogy. *Theory into Practice, 34*(3), *Culturally Relevant Teaching*, 159–165.

Ladwig, J. G., & McPherson, A. (2017). The anatomy of ability. *Curriculum Inquiry, 47*(4), 344–362. https://doi.org/10.1080/03626784.2017.1368352

Lavrijsen, J., & Nicaise, I. (2015). New empirical evidence on the effect of educational tracking on social inequalities in reading achievement. *European Educational Research Journal*, 14(3–4), 206–221.

Lawrence-Brown, D., & Sapon-Shevin, M. (2014). *Condition critical: Key principles for equitable and inclusive education.* Teachers College Press.

Leonardo, Z., & Broderick, A. (2011) Smartness as property: A critical exploration of intersections between whiteness and disability studies. *Teachers College Record, 113*(10), 2206–2232.

Library of Congress (n.d.). *School segregation and integration.* Civil Rights History Project. Retrieved August 3, 2021 from https://www.loc.gov/collections/civil-rights-history-project/articles-and-essays/school-segregation-and-integration/

Lovern, L. L., & Locust, C. (2013). Native American Communities on Health and Disability: A borderland dialogues. Palgrave MacMillan

MacDonald, D. B., & Hudson, G. (2012). The genocide question and Indian residential schools in Canada. *Canadian Journal of Political Science / Revue canadienne de science politique (45)*2, 427–449.

Madden, B. (2019) A de/colonizing theory of truth and reconciliation education, *Curriculum Inquiry, (49)*3, 284–312. https://doi.org/10.1080/03626784.2019.1624478

Malcomson, T. (2008). Applying selected SRV themes to the eugenic movement in Canada & the United States, 1890–1972. *The SRV Journal, 3*(1), 34–51.

Mahn, H. (1999). Vygotsky's methodological contribution to sociocultural theory. *Remedial and Special Education, 20*(6), 341–350. https://doi.org/10.1177/074193259902000607

Mansfield, K. C. (2015). Giftedness as property: Troubling whiteness, wealth, and gifted education in the United States. *International Journal of Multicultural Education, 17*(1), 1–18.

Martin, J. L., (n.d.). Understanding the modern menu of public education services for struggling learners: RTI Action Network. http://www.rti-network.org/connect/discussion/topic?id=521

Mas, J. M., Dunst, C. J., Balcells-Balcells, A., Garcia-Ventura, S., Giné, C., & Cañadas, M. (2019). Family-centered practices and the parental well-being of young children with disabilities and developmental delay. *Research in Developmental Disabilities, 94*, 1–13. https://doi.org/10.1016/j.ridd.2019.103495

Matthewes, S. H. (2018). Better together? Heterogeneous effects of tracking on student achievement. DIW Discussion Papers, No. 1775, Deutsches Institut für Wirtschaftsforschung (DIW).

Mazel, S. (2020a). 5-month-old baby. *What to expect* [Blog]. https://www .whattoexpect.com/first-year/month-by-month/month-$2aspx

Mazel, S. (2020b). 12-month-old baby. *What to expect* [Blog]. https:// www.whattoexpect.com/toddler/12-month-old/

MCauley, S. (2018, Winter). Culturally relevant and responsive pedagogy in the early years: It's never too early! *ETFO Voice: Magazine of the Elementary Teachers' of Toronto Federation.* https://etfovoice.ca/feature/ never-too-early

McClure, C. T. (2007). Ability grouping and acceleration in gifted education. *District Administration, 43*(8), 24–25.

Mingus, M. (2011). Changing the framework: Disability Justice. Leaving Evidence. https://leavingevidence.wordpress.com/2011/02/12/ changing-the-framework-disability-justice/

Mitchell, D. (2010). *Education that fits: Review of international trends in the education of students with special educational needs.* University of Canterbury. https://www.educationcounts.govt.nz/publications/ special_education/education-that-fits-review-of-international-trends -in-the-education-of-students-with-special-educational-needs

Mitchell, D. (2014). *What really works in special and inclusive education: Using evidence-based teaching strategies.* (2nd ed.). Routledge.

Mitchell, D. (2015). *Education that fits: Review of international trends in the education of students with special educational needs.* (2nd ed.). University of Canterbury. https://www.education.vic.gov.au/Documents/ about/department/psdlitreview_Educationthatfits.pdf

Mutcherson, K. (2017). Disability, procreation, and justice in the United States, *Laws, 6*(27), 1–15. https://doi.org/10.3390/laws6040027

National Center for Education Statistics (2018). Table 204.30. *Children 3 to 21 years old served under Individuals with Disabilities Education Act (IDEA), Part B, by type of disability: Selected years, 1976–77 through 2017– 18.* https://nces.ed.gov/programs/digest/d18/tables/dt18_204.30.asp

Ne'eman, A. (2020, March 23). "I will not apologize for my needs." Even in a crisis, doctors should not abandon the principle of nondiscrimination [Op-ed]. *The New York Times* https://www.nytimes.com/2020/03/23/ opinion/coronavirus-ventilators-triage-disability.html

Oakes, J. (2005). *Keeping track: How schools structure inequality.* Yale University Press.

O'Connor, C., & Fernandez, S. D. (2006). Race, class, and disproportionality: Reevaluating the relationship between poverty and special education placement. *Educational Researcher, 35*(6), 6–11.

Organisation for Economic Co-operation and Development (OECD). (2012). Does money buy strong performance in PISA? PISA in Focus 13. Retrieved from https://www.oecd.org/pisa/pisaproducts/pisainfocus/49685503.pdf

Ontario Education Act, R.S.O. 1990, c. E.2. https://www.ontario.ca/laws/statute/90e02

Ontario Human Rights Commission. (2018). *Policy on accessible education for students with disabilities.* http://www.ohrc.on.ca/en/policy-accessible-education-students-disabilities

Ontario Human Rights Commission. (2019). Right to Read: public inquiry into human rights issues affecting students with reading disabilities. http://www.ohrc.on.ca/en/right-read-public-inquiry-on-reading-disabilities

Ontario Ministry of Education. (2004). The Individual Education Plan (IEP): A resource guide. http://www.edu.gov.on.ca/eng/general/elemsec/speced/guide/resource/iepresguid.pdf

Ontario Ministry of Education. (2010). *Growing success: Assessment, evaluation, and reporting in Ontario Schools.* http://www.edu.gov.on.ca/eng/policyfunding/growSuccess.pdf

Ontario Ministry of Education. (2017). *Special education in Ontario: Kindergarten to grade 12—Policy and resource guide* [Draft]. http://www.edu.gov.on.ca/eng/document/policy/os/2017/SpecEdFinal2018.pdf

Parekh, G. (2013). *The case for inclusive education* (Report no. 12/13–09). Toronto District School Board.

Parekh, G. (2014). *Social citizenship and disability: Identity, belonging, and the structural organization of education* [Doctoral dissertation], York University, Ontario: Canada].

Parekh, G. (2017). The tyranny of ability. Curriculum Inquiry, *47*(4), 337-343.

Parekh, G. (2019). *Transformative action towards equity: Strategic remodeling of special education programming to support students' academic and social development* [Research report]. York University.

Parekh, G. (2020). How inclusive do we really want to be? A critical exploration of the Toronto District School Board's Special and Inclusive Education Policies and Outcomes. In S. Winton & G. Parekh (Eds.), *Critical perspectives on education policy and schools, families and communities* (pp. 123–140). Information Age.

Parekh, G., & Brown, R. (2019). Changing lanes: The relationship between special education placement and students' academic futures. *Politics of Education Yearbook, 33*(1), 111–135. https://doi.org/10.1177/0895904818812772

Parekh, G., & Brown, R. (2020). Naming and claiming: The tension between institutional and self-identification of disability. *Canadian Journal of Disability Studies, 9*(50), 346–379.

Parekh, G., Brown, R. S., & Robson, K. (2018). The social construction of giftedness: The intersectional relationship between whiteness, economic privilege, and the identification of gifted. *Canadian Journal of Disability Studies, 7*(2), 1–33.

Parekh, G., Brown, R. S., & Zheng, S. (2018). Learning Skills, system equity and implicit bias within Ontario, Canada. *Educational Policy, 35*(3), 395–421.

Parekh, G., Brown R. S., & Zheng, S. (2021, April). Learning and re-learning: A study of Ontario's Learning Skills and perceptions of student capacity [Virtual presentation]. Ontario Public Supervisory Officers' Association.

Parekh, G., Killoran, I., & Crawford, C. (2011). The Toronto connection: Poverty, perceived ability, and access to education equity. *Canadian Journal of Education, 34*(3), 249–279.

Parekh, G. & Underwood, K. (2015). *Inclusion: Creating school and classroom communities where everyone belongs* (Report No. 15/16–09). Toronto: Toronto District School Board.

Parekh, G., & Underwood, K. (2020, May 14). *Coronavirus crisis shows ableism shapes Canada's long-term care systems for people with disabilities.* The Conversation. https://theconversation.com/coronavirus-crisis-shows-ableism-shapes-canadas-long-term-care-for-people-with-disabilities-137478

Parens, E. (Ed.) (2006). *Surgically shaping children: Technology, ethics, and the pursuit of normality.* Johns Hopkins University Press.

Poole, J., Jivraj, T., Arslanian, A., Bellows, K., Chiasson, S., Hakimy, H., Pasini, J., & Reid, J. (2012). Sanism, "mental health" and social work/education: A review and call to action. *Intersectionalities, 1,* 20–36.

Posey, A. (n.d.). *Universal design for learning (UDL): A teacher's guide.* Understood. https://www.understood.org/en/school-learning/for-educators/universal-design-for-learning/understanding-universal-design-for-learning

Quan, D. & James, C. E. (2017). Unlocking student potential through data: Final report. Toronto, Ontario, Canada: Ontario Ministry of Education.

Redding, C., & Grissom, J. A. (2021). *Do students in gifted programs perform better? Linking gifted program participants to achievement and non-achievement outcomes* [Presentation]. American Educational Research Association Annual Meeting.

Regan, P. (2010). *Unsettling the settler within: Indian residential schools, truth telling, and reconciliation in Canada.* UBC Press.

Reid, L., Parekh, G., & Lattanzio, R. (2020). Relic of the past: Identification, placement and review committees in Ontario's education system. *Canadian Journal of Educational Administration and Policy, 194*

Reid, D. K., & Knight, M. G. (2006) Disability justifies exclusion of minority students: A critical history grounded in disability studies, educational researcher, *35*(6), 18–23.

Rix, J., & Ingham, N. (2021). The impact of education selection according to notions of intelligence: A systematic literature review. *International Journal of Education Research Open, 2*(2), 1–9.

Rossiter, K., & Rinaldi, J. (2018). *Institutional violence and disability: Punishing conditions.* Routledge

Rubin, B. C. (2006), Tracking and detracking: Debates, evidence, and best practices for a heterogeneous world. *Theory Into Practice, 45*(1), 4–14. https://doi.org/10.1207/s15430421tip4501_2

Ryan, K. F. (2000). *A thumb on the scale: Biological determinism and the essays of Stephen Jay Gould* (Publication 811) [Master's thesis, New Jersey Institute of Technology]. Digital Commons@New Jersey Institute of Technology. https://digitalcommons.njit.edu/theses/811

ShadowWalker, D. (n.d.). Vygotsky and Indigenous cultures: Centuries of language centered learning. http://www.u.arizona.edu/~deprees/finalpaper.pdf

Shapiro, E. (2019, January 8). "I love my skin!" Why Black parents are turning to Africentric schools. *The New York Times*, https://www.nytimes.com/2019/01/08/nyregion/Africentric-schools-segregation-brooklyn.html

Shorelight Team. (2021). US vs Canadian universities: Study in USA. https://shorelight.com/student-stories/us-vs-canadian-universities-or-study-in-usa/

Sins Invalid (n.d). *Mission and vision*. https://www.sinsinvalid.org/about-us

Skiba, R., Poloni-Staudinger, L., Gallini, S., Simmons, A., & Feggins-Azziz, R. (2006). Disparate access: The disproportionality of African American students with disabilities across educational environments. *Exceptional Children, 72*(4), 411–424.

Slee, R. (2009). The inclusion paradox. *The Routledge international handbook to critical education*, 177. Retrieved from http://go.utlib.ca/cat/8775089

Sloan, K. (2013). The fallacy of intelligence and genetic determinism. The Centre for bioethics and culture network. https://www.cbc-network.org/2013/05/the-fallacy-of-intelligence-and-genetic-determinism/

Smaller, H. (2014). Streaming in Ontario schools. In Clandfield, D., Curtis, B., Galabuzi, G. E., Gaymes San Vincente, A., Livingstone, D., & Smaller, H. (Eds.), *Restacking the deck: Streaming by class, race, and gender in Ontario schools* (pp. 77–112). Our Schools/Our Selves.

Smith, P. (2004). Whiteness, normal theory, disability studies. Disability Studies Quarterly, *24*(2), https://dsq-sds.org/article/view/491/668

Starr, P. (1982). *The social transformation of American medicine: The rise of a sovereign profession and the making of a vast industry*. Basic Books.

State of Nevada Department of Education. (n.d.). Special Education Advisory Committee (SEAC). Overview. https://doe.nv.gov/Boards_Commissions_Councils/Special_Education_Advisory_Committee_(SEAC)/

Statistics Canada. (2017, November 29). *Ontario [Province] and Canada [Country]* (table). *Census profile*. 2016 Census. Statistics Canada Catalogue no. 98-316-X2016001.

Steenbergen-Hu, S., Makel, M., & Olszewski-Kubilius, P. (2016). What one hundred years of research says about the effects of ability grouping and acceleration on K–12 students' academic achievement: Findings of two second-order meta-analyses. *Review of Educational Research, 86*(4), 849–899. Retrieved August 4, 2021, from http://www.jstor.org/stable/44668238

Stephenson, B. (1978, December 15). "Special education" Ontario, legislative assembly, Official Report of Debates (Hansard), 31st Parliament, 2nd Session. http://hansardindex.ontla.on.ca/ hansardeissue/31-2/ 1152.htm

Stevenson, V. (2021). 'They let them die' at Quebec's worst-hit long-term care homes, union rep tells coroner. Canadian Broadcasting Corporation. https://www.cbc.ca/news/canada/montreal/sainte-dorothee-inquest-agicide-1.6075770

Stoeger, H. (2009). The history of giftedness research. *International handbook on giftedness* (pp. 17–38). https://doi.org/10.1007/978-1-4020-6162-2 2

Stonefish, T., & Lafreniere, K. D. (2015). Embracing diversity: The dual role of gay-straight alliances. *Canadian Journal of Education/Revue Canadienne De l'éducation, 38*(4), 1–27. Retrieved from https:// journals.sfu.ca/cje/index.php/cje-rce/article/view/1854

Storer, E. (2008). Gay-Straight Alliances. Outhistory: It's about time! https://outhistory.org/exhibits/show/queer-youth-campus-media/high-school/gay-straight-alliances

Subini, A., & Morrison, D. (2018). Identifying dysfunctional education ecologies: A DisCrit analysis of bias in the classroom. *Equity & Excellence in Education, 51*(2), 114–131. https://doi.org/10.1080/10665684 .2018.1496047

Terman, L. M. (1916). *The measurement of intelligence*. Houghton Mifflin.

Tieso, C. L. (2003). Ability grouping is not just tracking anymore. *Roeper Review, 26*(1), 29–36.

Tilley, E., Walmsley, J., Earle, S., & Atkinson, D. (2012). "The silence is roaring": Sterilization, reproductive rights and women with intellectual disabilities. *Disability & Society, 27*(3), 413–426. https://doi .org/10.1080/09687599.2012.654991

To, J. (2021). De-streaming in the Toronto District School Board. Guest lecture on inclusive practice and mathematics. York University.

To, J., Lloyd, E., Bacchus, N., & Gaymes San Vicente, A. (2017). *Restructured pathways: Addressing streaming from grades 1 to 12 in the Toronto District School Board*. Toronto District School Board.

Tomlinson, C. A. (2001). *How to differentiate in mixed-ability classrooms* (2nd ed.). Association for Supervision and Curriculum Development.

Tomlinson, C. A., & Imbeau, M. B. (2010). *Leading and managing a differentiated classroom*. ASCD Member Books. http://www1.kdsi.org/strategicpd/wp-content/uploads/2014/09/Differentiated-Classroom.pdf

Toronto District School Board (2015). *The 2013–2014 Environmental scan of the Toronto District School Board*. Retrieved from http://www.tdsb.on.ca/Portals/0/AboutUs/Research/2013-2014TDSBEnvironmentalScan.pdf

Toronto District School Board. (2020). Africentric alternative school. https://schoolweb.tdsb.on.ca/africentricschool

Toulouse, P.R. (2018). *Truth and reconciliation in Canadian schools*. Portage & Main Press.

Truth and Reconciliation Commission of Canada (TRC). (2015a). *Truth and Reconciliation Commission of Canada: Calls to action*. http://nctr.ca/assets/reports/Calls_to_Action_English2.pdf

Truth and Reconciliation Commission of Canada (TRC). (2015b). *Honouring the truth, reconciling for the future summary of the final report of the Truth and Reconciliation Commission of Canada* http://www.trc.ca/assets/pdf/Honouring_the_Truth_Reconciling_for_the_Future_July_23_2015.pdf

Understood Team. (n.d.). *The difference between IEPs and 504 plans*. Understood. https://www.understood.org/en/school-learning/special-services/504-plan/the-difference-between-ieps-and-504-plans

Underwood, K. (2013). Everyone is welcome: Inclusive early childhood education and care. Ministry of Education. Retrieved from https://pdf4pro.com/cdn/everyone-is-welcome-inclusive-early-childhood-education-5b7c89.pdf

Underwood, K., & Parekh, G. (2020). *Child care after the coronavirus pandemic should be more inclusive of children with disabilities*. The Conversation. https://theconversation.com/child-care-after-the-coronavirus-pandemic-should-be-more-inclusive-of-children-with-disabilities-141172

Underwood, K., Frankel, E., Parekh, G., & Janus, M. (2019). Transitioning work of families: Understanding trans-institutional power in early childhood programs and services. *Exceptionality Education International, 29*(3), (135–153).

Underwood, K., Church. K., & van Rhijn, T. (2020). Responsible for normal: The contradictory work of families. In S. Winton & G. Parekh (Eds.), *Critical perspectives on education policy and schools, families and communities.* Information Age.

United Nations. (1966). International Covenant on Economic, Social and Cultural Rights. https://www.ohchr.org/en/professionalinterest/pages/cescr.aspx

United Nations. (2006). Convention on the rights of persons with disabilities (CRPD). https://www.un.org/development/desa/disabilities/convention-on-the-rights-of-persons-with-disabilities.html

United Nations. (2016). General comment no. 4. Article 24. Right to inclusive education. https://www.ohchr.org/Documents/HRBodies/CRPD/GC/RighttoEducation/CRPD-C-GC-4.doc

United States Holocaust Memorial Museum. (2020). *Euthanasia program and Aktion T4.* Retrieved August 3, 2021 from ttps://encyclopedia.ushmm.org/content/en/article/euthanasia-program

United States Department of Education. (2017). IDEA: Individuals with Disabilities Education Act. Retrieved August 3, 2021 from ttps://sites.ed.gov/idea/regs/c/d

United States Department of Education. (2020). Protecting students with disabilities. https://www2.ed.gov/about/offices/list/ocr/504faq.html

Valle, J., & Connor, D. J. (2010). *Rethinking dis/ability: A dis/ability studies guide to inclusive practices.* New York, NY: McGraw-Hill.

Vintimilla, C. D. (2018). Encounters with a pedagogista. *Contemporary issues in early childhood, 19*(1), 20–30.

Wahlsten, D. (1997). Leilani Muir versus the philosopher king: Eugenics on trial in Alberta, *Genetica, 99,* 185–198

Waltz, M., & Schippers, A. (2020). Politically disabled: Barriers and facilitating factors affecting people with disabilities in political life within the European Union. *Disability & Society, 36*(4), 517–540 https://doi.org/10.1080/09687599.2020.1751075

Warne, R. (2019). An evaluation (and vindication?) of Lewis Terman: What the father of gifted education can teach the 21st century. *Gifted Child Quarterly*, *63*(1), 3–21. https://doi.org/10.1177/0016986218799433

Washington Office of Superintendent of Public Instruction. (n.d). *Initial evaluations, reevaluations, and independent educational evaluations*.   https://www.k12.wa.us/student-success/special-education/guidance-families-special-education-washington-state/evaluations

Watters, H. (2015). *Truth and Reconciliation chair urges Canada to adopt UN declaration on Indigenous peoples*. CBC. Retrieved from http://www.cbc.ca/news/politics/truth-and-reconciliation-chair-urges-canada-to-adopt-un-declaration-on-indigenous-peoples-1.3096225

Weisberger, M. (2021). Remains of more than 1,000 Indigenous children found at former residential schools in Canada. Live Science. https://www.livescience.com/childrens-graves-residential-schools-canada.html

Westoll, N. (2017, May 16). *Violence in the classroom: Ontario mother of student with special needs speaks out*. Global News. https://globalnews.ca/news/3456448/ontario-durham-classroom-safety-update/

Whyte, K. P., (2016, April 17) *Indigenous experience, environmental justice and settler colonialism*. Social Science Research Network. https://doi.org/10.2139/ssrn.2770058

Withers, A. J. (2012). *Disability politics and theory*. Fernwood Publishing: Halifax & Winnipeg

Woolford, A (2015). *This benevolent experiment: Indigenous boarding schools, genocide, and redress in Canada and the United States*. University of Nebraska Press.

World Population Review (n.d.). Website: Ontario. https://worldpopulationreview.com/canadian-provinces/ontario-population

Index

ability
    assessment of, xv
    as central feature of meritocracy, 29
    as constructed and organized in
        schools, 21–39
    critically examining, xiii–xiv
    defined, 5–6
    described, xiii–xiv, 33
    "fixedness" associated with levels of,
        34–35
    forms of, xv
    hierarchies of, 6–7, 77–92. *see also*
        under academic streaming;
        academic tracking
    notions on, 3, 85–91
    perceived. *see* perceived ability
    promoting development of, xiv
    schooling and, 5–7
    in schools. *see* ability in schools
    schools response to and organization of
        students by, xiv–xv
    students organized by, 57–102
    teacher education programs in
        addressing, 21–23
    testing related to, 23–26. *see also*
        ability testing
    thinking through, 1–55
    "tyranny of," xv
    views of, 3–4
ability-based decisions, xiv
ability-grouping, 68–71
    benefits of, 35
    criticisms of, 34–35
    dangers of, 133
    district data and, 71–73, 72*f*
    hierarchy in schools related to, 37–38,
        37*n*
    negative consequences to students'
        learning related to, 34
    in special education identification,
        68–71
    stigma related to, 35–38
    trauma related to, 36–37
ability in schools
    described, xv–xvi
    organizational decisions based on, xiv–xv
    uses for, xiii–xiv
ability neutrality
    homogeneity and, 42–44
    myth of, 42–44
    whiteness and, 42–44
ability-related oppression, 11
ability testing
    history of, 23–26
    strategies in countering oppressive
        effects of, 27–28, 100–102

sharing instructions in, 127–28
TEDx Talk on, 109
texts in, 128
inclusive activity/assignment
designing, 125–26
inclusive classroom, 108–9
inclusive education, 105–15
critical approaches to, 105–15. *see also*
inclusion
described, 108–9
what it's not, 109–10
inclusive pedagogy and practice, 117–30.
See also under inclusion
independent education evaluations
(IEEs), 63
Indigenous perspectives
child development understandings of, 32
disability-related approaches by, 3–4
in residential schools, 139–41
individual education plan/program (IEP),
61–62, 82, 114
components of, 61–62
creation of, 61
functions of, 61–62
in US and Ontario, 61
Individuals with Disabilities Education
Act (IDEA), 105, 132
described, 59
disability categories under, 63
injustice(s)
disability-related, 25
institutional identification
implications of processes, 65–68
self-identification vs., 14, 64–65
instruction(s)
differentiated, 124
direct, 124–25
sharing, 127–28
Integrated Family Service Plans, 59
intelligence
measurement of, 26

normative, 25
intelligence quotient (IQ)
in student placement in special
education programs, 26
intelligence testing
development and promotion of, 26
psychometric, 23
in special education practices, 26–27
Intelligence Quotient (IQ) test(s), 24
weaponization of, 25
IPRC. *See* Identification, Placement and
Review Committee (IPRC)
IQ. *See* Intelligence Quotient (IQ)

"judgmental" categories, 66
justice
disability-related implications, xv,
14–15, 143–46
education-related implications,
143–46
GSAs and, 142–44
importance of, 138–43
LGBTQ2S+ community and, 142–43
modeling commitment to, 117–30
setting new conditions for, 131–46. *see
also* right(s)
truth and, 139–41
justice movement(s), 65
Africentric schooling, 141–42, 141*n*
disability justice, xv, 9, 14–16, 101, 111,
114, 131, 138, 141–145

learning environment
defined, 124
Learning Skills
evaluation of, 46–51, 47*f*–51*f*
types of, 46–51, 47*f*–51*f*
Lesbian, Gay, Bisexual, Transgender,
Queer, Two-Spirit + (LGBTQ2S+)
community
justice and, 142–43

About the Author

Gillian Parekh, PhD, is an Associate Professor and Canada Research Chair in Disability Studies in Education within the Faculty of Education at York University. Through her research on special education and academic streaming, her work explores how schools construct and respond to disability.

For Product Safety Concerns and Information please contact our
EU representative GPSR@taylorandfrancis.com Taylor & Francis
Verlag GmbH, Kaufingerstraße 24, 80331 München, Germany